From London

The British Council
in association with the
Scottish National Gallery of Modern Art
1995-1996

An exhibition organised by The British Council
in association with the Scottish National Gallery of Modern Art

Scottish National Gallery of Modern Art, Edinburgh
1 July – 5 September 1995

Musée National d'Histoire et d'Art, Luxembourg
22 September – 5 November 1995

Musée cantonal des Beaux-Arts, Lausanne
16 November 1995 – 31 January 1996

Fundació Caixa de Catalunya, La Pedrera, Barcelona
16 February – 7 April 1996

Exhibition selected by Richard Calvocoressi
Exhibition officer: Robert McPherson (BC)
Exhibition assistants: Kate Rhodes (BC) and Sarah Walker (BC)
Catalogue edited by Richard Calvocoressi and Philip Long (SNGMA)

Illustrations © The artists; the estate of Francis Bacon; Mrs Michael
Andrews and Bruce Bernard
Texts © The authors and The British Council

Catalogue published jointly by The British Council and the
Scottish National Gallery of Modern Art and available from
The British Council, 11 Spring Gardens, London SWIA 2BN

ISBN 0 86355 288 9

Designed and typeset in Caslon by Dalrymple
Printed and bound by BAS Printers Ltd

Cover illustration: detail from *Portrait of a Man
Walking Down Steps* by Francis Bacon (no. 5)

Wheeler's Restaurant, Old Compton Street, Soho 1962
left to right: Tim Behrens, Lucian Freud, Francis Bacon, Frank Auerbach, Michael Andrews
photo: John Deakin

Preface

IS THERE SUCH a thing as a 'School of London'? And if so, what is it? By looking at the work of six artists who have shown an unwavering commitment to figurative painting in a period largely characterised by indifference to it, this exhibition attempts to suggest some answers. R. B. Kitaj, who coined the term, referred to the 'world-class' painters he found around him in London as 'a herd of differing loners', so it should come as no surprise that the work of all six looks remarkably different. Yet they knew and encouraged one another, often painted each other, sometimes studied and frequently associated together in a city which provided the freedom not to conform, so that each might develop away from institutional pressure and find his own voice. That they were often in one another's company is shown by John Deakin's photograph on p. 6. In fact, this photograph is something of a fake, since Deakin had been trying to get them together, unsuccessfully, for a group photograph on a number of occasions. In the end, he had to bribe them with the promise of dinner at Wheeler's, a relatively expensive restaurant at a time when none of them, with the exception of Bacon, had much money. You can tell from the unpeeled foil and unsullied plates that there wasn't any real eating or drinking going on. And perhaps this is symbolic of the group status accorded to them: willing participants in a sympathetic plot which each will go away afterwards to pursue in his own singular and inimitable manner.

The exhibition has been selected by Richard Calvocoressi, Keeper of the Scottish National Gallery of Modern Art, Edinburgh, who worked with all five artists from the outset and who received their fullest co-operation. The organisation of the exhibition has been undertaken with customary flair by Robert McPherson, with assistance from Kate Rhodes and Sarah Walker. In each of the four cities in which the exhibition has been shown we are indebted to the help of a number of individuals and institutions.

In Edinburgh thanks are due to Philip Long, Margaret Mackay and Alice O'Connor of the Scottish National Gallery of Modern Art, Edinburgh; in Luxembourg to Andrea Addison, Nicholas Elam CMG, Jean-Luc Koltz and Paul Reiles, Director of the Musée National d'Histoire et d'Art, Luxembourg; in Lausanne to David Beattie CMG; Galerie Beyeler, Basle; BT British Telephone Ltd; Gilbert de Botton; Lipton-Sais; Philip J Priestley; Patrick Schaefer;

Fondation Sirina, Vaduz; Stanley Thomas Johnson Foundation; Stedelijk Museum, Amsterdam; Thomas Ammann Fine Art AG, Zurich and Jörg Zutter, Director of the Musée cantonal des Beaux-Arts, Lausanne and in Barcelona to José Luis Giménez-Frontin, Director of La Pedrera, Louise Higham and Marta Canals.

Most importantly, we should like to take this opportunity to thank the lenders to this exhibition, many of them private individuals who wish to remain anonymous, for responding so generously to our requests to borrow works. The artists' galleries have also been extremely helpful and we should like to single out for special thanks: Valerie Beston and Kate Austen of Marlborough Fine Art, London; David Case, Alexandra Wettstein and Sarah Staughton of Marlborough Graphics, London; Robin Vousden of Anthony d'Offay Gallery, London; Duncan MacGuigan of Acquavella Galleries, New York; and Peter Goulds and Kristin Rey of L. A. Louver Gallery, Venice, California. We should also like to record our gratitude to June Andrews, David Alston, Hans Rasmus Astrup, Kaare Berntsen, Hans-Jakob Brun, Caroline Douglas, Jane Farrington, Brenda Garfield, Linda Homfray, Hugues Joffre, Tomas Llorens, Maria de Peverelli, Lord and Lady Rothschild, Elizabeth Smallwood, Leo Walsh and Baroness Willoughby de Eresby for their unstinting support.

The main essay in the catalogue is by the art historian and critic David Cohen. His imaginative and stimulating text places the School of London painters within a broader European context, in particular that of post-war existentialist thought, and suggests a number of interesting connections between their work. Bruce Bernard has provided an engaging and highly personal memoir, accompanied by his own photographs, of his friendships with four of the artists, which offers a unique insight into their personalities and working methods. We are grateful to both authors for their contributions.

Finally, it is a sad duty to record the death of Michael Andrews in July 1995, two weeks after the opening of the exhibition in Edinburgh. The most idiosyncratic of all the 'School of London' artists, his final painting of the Thames is a reflection on time and tide, on the great river that binds and divides the people of London, on history in the present tense. If the 'School of London' label means anything, it is surely that painting communicates one man's lived experience of the world more succinctly, vividly and lastingly than any of the 'new media' that now threaten to eclipse it as we approach the millennium.

ANDREA ROSE
Head of Visual Arts
The British Council

From London

RICHARD CALVOCORESSI

WITH THE EXCEPTION of Francis Bacon, who was born before the First World War and who died in 1992, the artists in this exhibition were born in the 1920s or early 1930s – that is to say, were in their late teens or early twenties when the Second World War ended. 1945 was the year that Bacon, already in his mid-thirties, first attracted public notice in London when his *Three Studies for Figures at the Base of a Crucifixion* was shown, to shocked visitors, at the Lefevre Gallery. Of a different generation, Bacon was at one time or another admired or emulated by the other five artists in this exhibition. All six, rightly or wrongly, have become identified in recent years as the nucleus of a so-called School of London. Even so, it is odd that this is the first occasion in the UK that they have been shown as a group. (The British Council's 1987–88 touring exhibition of the same six, *A School of London*, was not seen in Britain.)

The term 'School of London' was coined by Kitaj in 1976 to denote a disparate collection of London-based artists united only in their (then) unfashionable dedication to the human form – what Kitaj called 'the most basic art-idea, from which so much great art has come'. Kitaj's pictorial language up to that date had been deliberately elliptical and allusive but a new interest in life drawing helped him develop a more integrated and heroic figure style, while retaining a preference for allegory and complex themes. Only works made since Kitaj's change of course in the mid-seventies are included in this exhibition. The title, *From London*, echoes the title of a painting from this important transitional period in Kitaj's work, which is also one of his most memorable portraits of London intellectuals.

For each of the six artists, London has provided as subjects a circle of (often mutual) friends, family and models. This exhibition includes portraits by Michael Andrews of fellow Slade student Tim Behrens (no. 35) and photographer John Deakin (no. 36), both of whom were also painted by Lucian Freud. The architect Colin St. John Wilson has been painted by Kitaj (no. 64) and Andrews. The photographer and journalist Bruce Bernard describes later in this catalogue the experience of being painted by Andrews and drawn by Frank Auerbach; he has also recently been painted by Freud. Most of the artists have made portraits of each other.

9

London also offers the seclusion needed to pursue an intensive engagement with the motif, whether figure or landscape. Of the six, only Kossoff was born and brought up in London, although all have lived (or lived) in the city for thirty years or more. Kossoff and Auerbach in particular have made London their subject, each registering in pulsating accretions of paint his knowledge of the buildings, open spaces and gritty street life of his neighbourhood. Auerbach has occupied the same studio in Camden Town for the past forty years and rarely leaves it. Both artists paint a small number of unglamorous motifs, each time seeing afresh and creating out of the local and transitory an enduring image of monumentality.

When we look at one of Freud's paintings, we are entering an even more enclosed world, beyond time, in which views of the outside are restricted to the occasional glimpse of seedy urban landscape through the studio window. *Wasteground with Houses, Paddington* (no. 14) is at once palpably real and eerily remote: a vision of deserted backs of houses with domestic rubbish that can be read as a portrait of its absent inhabitants. Freud's naked figures, some of which conversely resemble the contours and rhythms of landscape, share a similar sense of dissociation and anonymity; and yet we also feel that we are there in the studio, uncomfortably close to the sitter. The more relaxed and vulnerable Freud's figures – for example, in the privacy of sleep – the stronger this feeling of intrusion becomes. Freud's clothed portraits are on the whole less intimate, their subjects tense and wary like cornered animals, eyes averted from the viewer's stare (no. 20).

Michael Andrews is the least studio-bound of the six artists. In 1977 he left London to live in the Norfolk countryside and for the next fifteen years was engaged in painting two major series of landscapes: of Scotland, where he has spent part of almost every summer since 1975, and of Ayers Rock in Australia, which he visited in 1983. He returned to live in London in 1992 and has recently completed two pictures of the River Thames at low tide: the first an image of primal flux, without horizon, in which paint (to adapt a phrase of Lucian Freud's) is made to work as mud and water; the second (no. 48), by contrast, an ethereal vision of immateriality.

Andrews's dry, self-effacing style is usually thought to be the most naturalistic of the School of London painters. Beneath the artist's dispassionate scrutiny, however, lies a subtle but disconcerting rearrangement of appearance to reflect his emotional response to the motif: 'what one sees with one's interpretation of what one sees' is how Andrews has defined reality. Certain passages of paint are the result of chance effects or the incorporation of actual substances found in the landscape. The compositions themselves compress and conflate different views recorded by the artist in photographs. Andrews synthesises information culled from a variety of sources.

R. B. Kitaj *From London (James Joll and John Golding)* 1975–76 Private collection

Andrews's early interest in individuals and groups has given way to a concern with what the artist calls 'habitats'. The Scottish and Australian pictures powerfully demonstrate his conception of a synoptic, historical landscape: although empty of people, it is charged with the presence of those who have helped to define it or give it significance, whether historical (no. 47) or spiritual (no. 40). The inter-relationship of man and his environment is Andrews's true subject.

Accidental effects and photography also stimulated Francis Bacon in his search for an authentic image of displaced modern man. 'I'm always hoping to deform people into appearance; I can't paint them literally', he once said. Bacon rejected literary interpretations of his imagery – for example, the idea that the contortions and convulsions of his isolated figures trapped in their bleak urban rooms are evocative of suffering, or symbolise the horror and violence of the twentieth century; instead, he pointed to 'the violence of reality itself'. It is certainly the case that on one level Bacon's paintings are profoundly private and ambiguous statements. This exhibition contains two of his portraits of George Dyer (nos. 4, 5), his lover and model for many years and the subject of some of his most poignant canvases. But on another level Bacon's achievement was to take archetypal subjects from literature, mythology and Christian iconography – the whole tradition of western culture – and recreate them in a form that reflects our secular but atrocity-conscious age. *Triptych inspired by the Oresteia of Aeschylus* (no. 6) invokes Bacon's favourite Greek tragedy, with its line spoken by one of the Furies that haunted him: 'The reek of human blood smiles out at me'. It is Bacon's most extraordinary late work and one of his undoubted masterpieces.

Critics have been tempted to identify an expressionist strain in School of London painting whereas in fact expressionism could not be further from the concerns of the artists in this exhibition. Bacon's earliest paintings were influenced by Picasso's work of the twenties when the latter was close to Surrealism. Bacon's use of the triptych format in several works and his interest in symmetry and architectural structure also suggest other, more classical sources of inspiration. Kitaj's early pictures would be unimaginable without the example of surrealist collage. His later, 'parable-pictures' (to use his own term) recall, if anyone, Max Beckmann, who was decidedly not an expressionist. The preoccupation with hallucinatory precision and detail in Freud's early work superficially resembles Magic Realist or *Neue Sachlichkeit* painting of the twenties, but more strongly evokes the sharp line and glacial finish of Northern Renaissance art. Even though Freud's brushstrokes have broadened and loosened over the years, leading to rougher and pastier surfaces, a portrait involves countless sittings and may include a number of visual conceits: his is a highly self-conscious art. Andrews's paintings are similarly the result of a process of observation, reasoning and adjustment, and can take months, sometimes years, to complete. The recent paintings of Auerbach and Kossoff, with their fluid swirls and drips of paint, look the most spontaneous and instinctive of the six. But behind them lies an accumulation and distillation of experience, involving drawings and numerous false starts. Self-discipline and artistic economy inform their work too.

If there is a single source of inspiration common to all six artists, it is that treatment of the great universal themes of human existence to be found in the paintings of the Old Masters, available to them in profusion every day of the year in London's National Gallery.

George Dyer at Knossos, June 1965
cf. Francis Bacon *Portrait of a Man Walking Down Steps* (no. 5)
photo: John Deakin

Interior of Frank Auerbach's studio
Cover illustration from *The Hard-Won Image* exhibition catalogue 1984
photo: Peter Wood

'Grand, Living and Quirky Forms'
Six Painters of the School of London

DAVID COHEN

IN THE CORNER of a painter's studio an easel displays what looks like, but is not, a completed canvas.[1] Preparatory drawings, and drawings after an Old Master, are pinned to the mottled, peeling wall. Above them is a photograph of a friend's work. An open art book balances precariously on a paint-spattered worktop among brushes, encrusted paint pots, and discarded newspapers.

This is the photograph on the cover of a Tate Gallery exhibition catalogue, *The Hard-Won Image: Traditional Method and Subject in Recent British Art* (1984).

Describing how a 1940s Giacometti catalogue galvanised his generation, the critic David Sylvester said 'It was like a talisman'.[2] It would be hard to think of a living artist more in awe of Giacometti than Frank Auerbach, whose North London studio has just been described.[3] For a younger generation of artists and devotees, the photo of Auerbach's heroically messy work space is also like a talisman. It is emblematic of artistic commitment, bravura and an unmodish sense that art entails existential struggle.

THIS EXHIBITION brings together work by six major painters of the post-war era. They all set out to make paintings with the weight and authority of the Old Masters, works packed with imagination and anchored in the observed world. The strongest bond between them might nonetheless be their common aloofness from prevailing fashions. R. B. Kitaj has described London painters as a 'herd of differing loners'.

The 'herd' assembled here have enjoyed friendships over several decades, and have shown in the same mixed exhibitions on several occasions. Again, it was Kitaj, the youngest of them, who came up with the name now commonly given to the group and the broader movement of which it is part: 'School of London'.[4] The others, so steeped in the conception of the artist as outsider, would never of their own accord have devised a label for themselves. That most of them have shunned invitations to join the Royal Academy is indicative of their attitude towards formal

15

associations.[5] But the idea of a 'School' has nonetheless washed with this group of fierce individualists and this attests to the depth of their comradeship. Although the notoriously abrasive Francis Bacon alienated each of his friends, these artists have often sat for one another, collected each others' work, and admiringly quoted each other.[6]

In coining the phrase 'School of London' Kitaj in fact reinforced, rather than challenged, an ethos of splendid isolation. In 1976 he selected *The Human Clay*, a seminal exhibition of works relating to the human figure, mostly drawings, by four-dozen contemporary artists, mostly British. Kitaj's selection ranged from obscure figure painters to well-known abstract or Pop artists and featured figure studies from artists who last drew as students, artists like himself who had rediscovered the figure mid-career, and artists for whom fidelity to a model or sitter has always been paramount. A quirky selection, but rather than a grand thesis to defend it Kitaj's foreword culminated in a rhetorical flourish:

> If some of the strange and fascinating personalities you may encounter here were given a fraction of the
> internationalist attention and encouragement reserved in this barren time for provincial and orthodox van-
> guardism, a School of London might become even more real than the one I have construed in my head.[7]

After *The Human Clay* exhibition of 1976 the international art world witnessed a resurgence of painting and figuration; London and Glasgow contributed to this phenomenon, and it is within this climate that some members of the group began to enjoy international reputations. But Neo-Expressionism meant different things to different people: the breaking of authoritarian taboos for some was nostalgia for lost order to others. Bombastic over-the-top painterliness was often carried out tongue-in-cheek, as a deconstruction of the very notion of originality. If pluralism was more tolerant towards those that went against the modernist grain, the downside was that talent was swamped where it had once been marginalised.

More recently, there has been a swing back to a hardline notion of avant-gardism, especially among a new generation. British artists are at the forefront of Neo-Conceptualism, the cool, dry, cerebral art which looks with renewed interest to the dominant movements of the 1960s and 1970s – Minimalism, Conceptualism and Pop art. These artists, who predominantly favour video, performance, appropriation and installation, are suspicious of traditional methods and subjects – unless they are to be debunked from within.

The neo-avant-gardism of the 1990s throws into sharper relief the polarized options that confronted, and were rejected by, the painters in this exhibition, between the devil of pure abstraction and the deep blue sea of conceptualist dematerialisation (happenings, installations etc). These extremes, pure form and idea art, are both results of reduction embarked upon in the conviction that 'less is more'.

The School of London is a school to the extent that it shares an abiding belief in the power of paint. To these men, less is less; the move towards distillation (not to be confused with compactness) represents diminution, impoverishment. What unites the pigment-loaded expressiveness of Auerbach and Kossoff, the fastidious, exacting representations of Freud and Andrews, the compelling, action-packed fictions of Bacon and Kitaj, is the conviction that – near as damn it – everything that matters can be said in paint. Touchstones of this conviction are to be found among the Old Masters. Most contemporary artists view art history as an image bank or a pool of formal devices and accomplishments. Whether in mockery or reverence, they feel remote from painters of the past. Not so the artists in this exhibition. Poussin, Rembrandt, Velázquez, Van Gogh are heroes, gods even, but friends and comrades too. Haunted and inspired in equal measure by what artist Helen Lessore called 'the great tradition',[8] they have copied and transcribed and vied with the masterpieces of humanistic, representational oil painting of the last half-dozen centuries.

When Auerbach is anxious about how he should finish a painting he visits the National Gallery, suggesting a hard-nosed and unsentimental attachment to the Old Masters. Kossoff draws great works 'to try to understand why certain pictures have a transforming effect on the mind'. Bacon has asked:

> Why after the great artists, do people ever try to do anything again? Only because, from generation to generation, through what the great artists have done, the instincts change. And, as the instincts change, so there comes a renewal of the feeling of how can I remake this thing once again more clearly, more exactly, more violently.[9]

If there is a common striving among the School of London painters for emulation of the greats without repetition, for saying everything in paint without capitulating to tried and tested pictorial solutions, a common result is awkwardness: formal tensions, compositional complications, stiltedness, abrasions, sometimes even the risk of cack-handedness. In an early review of the work of Michael Andrews, David Sylvester noted the element of awkwardness, which he partly related to 'that endearingly unprofessional uneasy look that is so common in English paintings of figure-subjects'. (Stubbs and Turner are cited as examples.) 'But Andrews's awkwardness', continues Sylvester,

> is not only an aspect of his pronounced Englishness. It is also the awkwardness of almost every modern painter who has not been content to solve his problems by simplifying them ... The modern artist who

aims at the *inclusiveness* of traditional European art runs up against the difficulty of recovering that inclusiveness without embracing what have become the clichés of the tradition, and the awkwardness arises from trying to have one without the other.[10]

The grand, living and quirky forms Auerbach has detected in late Sickert relate to an awkwardness of this order.

Sickert, a powerful influence on all of the artists in this show (see illustration p.20), once declared of the Old Masters: 'We have their blood in our veins.' Quoting these words in the catalogue of his *Artist's Eye* selection at the National Gallery, R. B. Kitaj wrote:

> I, for one, *feel* like a Post-Impressionist. Whenever I climb the steps at the home of depictive art in Trafalgar Square [the National Gallery], turn right and approach the large Seurat riverbank [*Bathers at Asnières* 1883–84], I feel like Alex Haley arriving in the Gambia. They were my people.[11]

Kitaj has a remarkable ability to conflate his reconnections with artistic and spiritual traditions, for instance figuration and Jewishness, as this quotation demonstrates. While to the older artists such protestations of personal identity would seem alien, Kitaj's conception of a supranational communion of artists across the ages has a particular bearing on the School of London (appropriately as the school first formed itself in his imagination). For while London is the capital of England, and while the artists draw strength from such English obstinacies of mind as empiricism and scepticism, only two of the six artists in this exhibition are English-born: Andrews and Kossoff, the latter the son of immigrants from war and revolution-traumatized Eastern Europe. Auerbach and Freud were Berliners, from which city they fled the Nazis as children. Bacon was from Ireland, and his childhood was set against 'the troubles' which accompanied that country's passage to independence. Kitaj himself was from Cleveland, Ohio. Although by his own confession he passed his childhood relatively oblivious of world events, the Holocaust is a subject which has come to haunt him, and he has played upon self-imagery of the wandering Jew in his paintings and writings. The most 'English' of the group, Michael Andrews, is nonetheless in spirit a 'Diasporist' (to use Kitaj's invented expression).[12] Andrews is on record as saying: 'I love the sense of homelessness and rootlessness. I'd like to die in a ditch.'[13]

All the artists in this exhibition were touched by the aura of existentialism, of which this last quote is redolent. Bacon attracted comparisons between his lonely, tortured men in their drab interiors (*huis clos*) and the writings of his contemporaries, Jean-Paul Sartre and fellow Anglo-Irishman Samuel Beckett.[14] Herbert Read, for one, related Bacon's 'symbols of a disintegrating world, of paranoiac consciousness' to Sartre. Read also famously referred to Freud as 'the Ingres of Existentialism', specifically thinking of the exquisitely wrought, polished depictions of anxious women, such as the 1947–48 portrait of the painter's first wife, eyes bulging in apprehension and clutching a rose (no. 11).[15]

Existentialism amounted to more than the depiction of *angst* or ennui for these artists. Andrews, Auerbach, Kitaj and Kossoff were students in the 1950s when the philosophy was at the height of its popularity and influence. Bacon and Freud may already have been confirmed in their outlooks but were no less prone to the new sense of peril engendered by the Bomb. The spectre of nuclear apocalypse, as much as the Holocaust which had claimed the lives of his family, may lurk behind Frank Auerbach's remark: 'It seems to me madness to wake up in the morning and do something other than paint considering the fact that one may not wake up the following morning'.[16]

While the impact of existentialism has been questioned by artists it is assumed to have affected,[17] each of the painters in this exhibition would probably identify with the notion of outsider. The idea of the artist 'born under Saturn', constitutionally inclined to melancholy and eccentric behaviour, has a long pedigree. Since the Romantics, this myth has consolidated into the belief that, because they are so sensitive to the very culture which alienates them, artists are natural critics of society and harbingers of change. Certain emblematic outsiders have featured in works by School of London artists: Bacon has painted a series devoted to Van Gogh and has taken the life-mask of William Blake as a subject; Auerbach has dedicated a series to Rimbaud (no. 54); and Kitaj has made Walter Benjamin – 'odd-ball marxist critic', lover of cities and victim of Fascism – the hero of one of his best-known canvases, *The Autumn of Central Paris (After Walter Benjamin)* 1972–73. Auerbach and Kossoff were pupils of David Bomberg, the expressionist painter ostracised by the establishment and avant-garde alike for his untimely convictions.

When the writer Colin Wilson published his 1956 analysis of literature and alienation, *The Outsider* (borrowing the title from Albert Camus), J. B. Priestley reviewed it together with John Osborne's play *Look Back in Anger* under the heading 'Angry Young Men'. This became the catchphrase for the gritty, gruff, nihilistic outlook of a new artistic generation. The 'angry young men' of painting were the group of realists championed by left-wing critic John Berger and known as the Kitchen Sink school.[18] These painters, who treated prosaic everyday subjects in a brutal, somewhat mannered naturalism (see Bratby illustration p.20), had previously shown at Helen Lessore's Beaux Arts Gallery, the same gallery with which School of London artists had strong ties.[19] While Kossoff often depicts inner city scenes – underground stations, schools, railway tracks – and Freud has painted industrial wasteground with chilling exactitude, all six artists are remote from social

Walter Richard Sickert (1860–1942)
*La Hollandaise c.*1906
Tate Gallery

William Coldstream (1908–87)
Reclining Nude 1953–54
Arts Council Collection

John Bratby (1928–92)
Table Top 1955
Portsmouth City Museums

Richard Hamilton (b.1922)
Self-Portrait 05.3.81e 1990
courtesy Anthony d'Offay Gallery © DACS

realism, from any need to comment moralistically on the lot of the working-classes. They may be existentialist in the value they place on immediacy and the present, in their sense of personal alienation, and (in the cases of Freud, Bacon and Auerbach) their radical remove from conventional, bourgeois lifestyles, but there is no begrudging class-consciousness in any of their work – as there certainly was in the 1950s generation of playwrights. The School of London is more interested in Ingres than anger.

There is no denying, however, that in the 1950s Andrews, Auerbach, Bacon, Freud and Kossoff inclined towards a sombre, lugubrious palette redolent of post-war austerity, to a *misérabliste* sensibility. Bacon withdrew from the garish backgrounds of those mid-1940s works which established his reputation (the orange of *Three Studies for Figures at the Base of a Crucifixion* 1944 and the pink of *Painting* 1946) for a period of restrained tonal painting, while Auerbach and Kossoff produced notoriously 'muddy' early works. Freud has continued throughout his career with a reined-in palette. While their visual attachment to the real world was generally apolitical (Kitaj is an exception here), the interests of these painters are remote from academic problems of perception and the language of art. Their aim is to make art which is compelling, inclusive and packed with life.

What is likely to induce a confusion between School of London painting and realism is the strong inclination of these artists towards the grubby, the mundane, in some of them indeed, the sordid. Sickert categorically asserted that 'The plastic arts are gross arts, dealing joyously with gross material facts. They call, in their servants, for a robust stomach and a great power of endurance ...'.[20] Whatever lofty themes or personal subjects School of London painters tackle, there is always the sense of the particular, the incidental, fiddly, itchy details. This is not to say they are obsessed with perceptual transcription, as for instance the Euston Road school of realists.[21] But it does indicate a fundamental attitude towards the experience of reality. Whatever stylistic licence the artists permit themselves in the depiction, for instance, of the body, one always senses actual bodily experience – weight, muscular tensions, internal workings. As to the sordid element, the 'rough trade' implied in Bacon's triptychs, the uncomfortable explicitness of Freud's nudes, and Kitaj's 'bitter undertaste' (to quote Flaubert) of brothel-life, all point to a pronounced urban orientation, to a Baudelarian sensibility. In their social hours, Bacon and, in younger days, Freud personified the role of dandy, while Kitaj often plays upon the figure of the *flâneur*, the city wanderer who spies on the crowd from within. In a funny sort of way, Michael Andrews's deer-stalker, roaming the Scottish Highlands and creeping up on his quarry, could be construed as a rustic *flâneur*.

Bacon and Kitaj stand apart from the others in their fascination with the visual trappings of modernity. Freud's studio by contrast, the setting for most of his compositions, could easily be taken for a nineteenth-century atelier, but Bacon and Kitaj, alive to the textures and forms of contemporary urban existence, are, in Baudelaire's phrase, 'painters of modern life'. In the 1930s Bacon had been a furniture designer: glass and tubular constructions are used to dramatic effect in his paintings. In Kitaj's pictures different modernist chairs become multifaceted symbols of cosmopolitanism, idealism, false comforts. These two painters would seem to connect with a strand in British art remote from the *angst* and ennui of the School of London, namely those modern social-scene painters who celebrate contemporary quirkiness in their art: Patrick Caulfield, David Hockney, Howard Hodgkin, and Allen Jones (all fellow students of Kitaj's at the Royal College of Art in the early 1960s). While *looking* very different from School of London painters, their concerns with an art of personal experience mediated through reality – 'gross material facts' in the consumer age – are contiguous. It could be argued that they form a second generation of the School, with Kitaj as bridge between the generations. However, a figure like Richard Hamilton, acknowledged as a father of British Pop, is almost a *doppelgänger* of the older artists, a *flâneur* made good who mocks the outsider image. For while he was a protégé of Bacon's, and an influence in his turn on Kitaj, his embrace of new technologies was total. In 1957, only half tongue-in-cheek, Hamilton prescribed new art as 'popular, transient, expendable, mass-produced, young, witty, sexy, gimmicky, glamorous and big business', about as opposite a definition as possible to the isolated, tenacious, psychologically intense, 'untimely' principles of the School of London.

IN HIS DRAMATIC painting *Whistler vs. Ruskin (Novella in Terre Verte, Yellow and Red)* 1992 Kitaj casts the protagonists of the famous art libel suit as boxers, basing his composition on the Ash Can painter George Bellows's *Dempsey and Firpo* 1924. Significantly, he paints himself in the neutral position of referee. As the case was about lack of finish and Whistler was an American-in-London, we might assume a certain bias, but the case is also about formalism ('Art for Art's Sake') versus art with moral purpose, higher content. The latter cause, with which Kitaj must sympathize, rests with Ruskin.

Historical dualities in art rarely map neatly onto later conflicts, but the form-content fight is alive in art today, and the School of London painters can be punched from either direction. As has already been suggested, a polarity has emerged in the last half-century between abstraction and dematerialisation, between the 'thing-itself' and the artist's ideas or performance. But just as abstract art has no monopoly on form – on the contrary, artists for whom paint is a vehicle for representation arguably make heavier demands of form – so too performance artists, or any artists only really interested in content or attitude, do not have privileged access to the world of ideas or the dramatic realm. School of London painters manage to compress emotion and observation into paint (or line in the case of graphic art) without slipping into the fetishisation of either material or process. At a time when artists are treated as performers, these are six personalities for whom any drama must be carried by the paint itself.

For Michel Leiris, 'Bacon's essential aim is not so much to produce a picture that will be an object worth looking at, as to use the canvas as a theatre of operations for the assertion of certain realities'.[22] His words directly recall the American critic Harold Rosenberg who wrote in 1952: 'At a certain moment the canvas began to appear to one American painter after another as an arena in which to act … What was to go on the canvas was not a picture but an event.'[23] Although Bacon was disdainful of such painters as Jackson Pollock and Willem De Kooning (De Kooning reputedly thought well of Bacon), these two Americans have been important, at various stages, for Auerbach, Kitaj, and Kossoff. What is interesting here is the way the abstract expressionists of the New York School, with their universalism and reductiveness, and the expressive figurative painters of the School of London, with their inclusiveness and enduring preference for the particular, shared existentialist concerns to the extent that a similar duality appears in their work, between process and result, theatre and 'the thing itself'. For the Americans, the drama of creativity was conveyed by gesture, by the weight and speed of the originating hand inscribed in the paint. Brushstrokes can similarly register the frenzy or violence of the expressive moment for Auerbach, Bacon, and Kossoff.

All the artists in this exhibition would balk at being described as 'theatrical'. While Bacon and Freud both achieved public notoriety for their bohemian lifestyles, neither has courted publicity, and indeed all six men have been professionally reserved in a way which is untypical of artists today. And yet in Bacon's pictures there are constant reminders of the illusory, artificial status of space. The gilt frames and glazing upon which he insisted evoke the proscenium arch of a theatre, while the triptych format recalls cinematic 'frames'. Certain titles make specific reference to dramatic works: *The Oresteia* of Aeschylus (no. 6); *Sweeney Agonistes* of T. S. Eliot. Mask and carnival is a marked theme in the paintings of Michael Andrews; some of his *Lights* series draw upon contemporary popular performers. As a student he appeared in two films by fellow Slade student Lorenza Mazzetti.[24] Kitaj has drawn inspiration from 'the beautiful craziness of Yiddish theatre'.[25]

Like Bacon, he has appropriated imagery from the silver screen. Before Frank Auerbach decided to become a painter he wanted to be an actor.

Lucian Freud, who was recently cast in the role of Louis XIV in a short film by two of his models, employed the Australian performance artist Leigh Bowery as model for some of his most ambitious male nudes.[26] Bowery cajoled an habitually reticent Freud into a candid interview for the underground journal *Lovely Jobley*.[27] When this was reprinted in a national newspaper nothing less than a collaborative performance by artist and model ensued for the benefit of photographer Bruce Bernard. In emulation of Gustave Courbet's monumental canvas of 1855, *The Artist's Studio*, the fleshy, gargantuan Bowery is posed naked like Courbet's muse, his modesty preserved by a white sheet, while the artist attends to his painting, a seated nude rear-view of Bowery. The painter's brush hovers somewhat pruriently at the parting of his model's buttocks. Bowery's pose in the painting is as art-historically informed as his performance before the camera, for it directly recalls Ingres's *Bather of Valpinçon* of 1808 in the Louvre.[28]

It may be objected that these escapades are merely an afternoon's high jinks after months of hard sitting and painting, hardly a footnote in the consideration of Freud's art. The point is, however, that the months of effort are *themselves* inscribed, if not into the painting then at least into the mystique surrounding it.

A modernist concern with process overturns the Old Master paradigm which asserts that it is the finished product alone which matters. In *Gillette or The Unknown Masterpiece* by Balzac, Frenhofer lectures the young Poussin as he corrects the efforts of the master Pourbus.

> You see, young fellow, it's the last stroke only which counts. Porbus [*sic*] made a hundred. I made only one.
>
> No one will thank us for what is underneath. That is something you should know.[29]

Whether they demand it or not, the creators of 'hard-won images' actually do receive acknowledgement, if not praise, for what is 'underneath': the scraped-down failed attempts of Auerbach and Kossoff, the rubbed-away or overpainted in Bacon and Freud, or the agonised hesitancy of Andrews and Kitaj. Multiple dates given to canvases by the latter two make plain that works can be several years in the making.

Bacon was a notorious destroyer of his own work: he managed to eradicate all his pre-1944 output save the few items in private collections, and many canvases subsequently. He once admitted that a 'finished' work is almost by definition one that his dealers managed to take away from the studio. That would be no criterion of absolute finality for Auerbach who has been known to retrieve sold pictures to scrape down and rework. Kitaj worked at *The Wedding* for four years

(1989–93), taking advice from the artists depicted in it, who include Hockney, Kossoff, Auerbach and Freud. 'In the end, instead of finishing it, I finished with it and gave it away to a deserving friend' (the friend being the Tate Gallery).[30]

Anxiety about finish lends existential edge to what would otherwise be a somewhat puritanical regard for the hard-won image. The way in which doubt or anxiety registers in the final product can vary enormously. Freud and Andrews, with their tentative, accumulated marks, recall Cézanne's *petites sensations*, while Bacon, Auerbach and Kossoff, for whom completion is mortgaged to a frenzied, expressive splurge – to the look of a gamble which has paid off – are closer in temperament to Giacometti. David Sylvester's analysis of Giacometti's *modus operandi* clearly holds for these London artists too:

> It is as if the process of creation consisted of a series of rehearsals and the final rehearsal was the performance, though the performer didn't know till afterwards that this rehearsal was to be the performance.[31]

Kitaj's doubt is not so evident in the actual marks upon the canvas – even in the 'old-age style' he has adopted in recent years, with its studied lack of finish. Instead, paradoxically, his doubt expresses itself as bravura: his bombastic association with 'the greats' is a performance deliberately meant only partially to conceal a permanent crisis of identity as acute in its way as the quiet self-doubt of his hero Cézanne.[32]

All the artists would identify passionately with Van Gogh's remark 'I would not like to have missed that error.' It invokes a painterly notion of doubt that transcends any ritualisation (theatricality) that might attend to their unusually self-punishing corrective procedures. In his characteristically understated and coded way, Michael Andrews encapsulates the whole philosophy of chance, error, doubt and finish with the observations 'culled' from deerstalking – a theme of recent pictures – recounted to Lawrence Gowing:

> 'It is no good, Mr Andrews', Alistair said, 'You cannot call back the bullet'. The friend with whom he was staying told him, 'You don't really know what stalking is about until you have missed.'[33]

FRANCIS BACON liked to quote the Symbolist poet Paul Valéry: 'What modern man wants is the grin without the cat, the sensation without the boredom of its conveyance.'[34]

The violence of his subject matter and the immediacy of its presentation assault the most hardened sensibility. But what is the status of 'violence' within his work, and indeed within his vocabulary? Andrew Sinclair, in his recent life of the artist, is convinced that Bacon's art reflects his violent times, a childhood in London during the Great War, Ireland during the troubles, and sexual coming of age in libertine Weimar Berlin, not to mention the universal calamities, Auschwitz and Hiroshima. 'He read the entrails of his half-century, pulverised them and vomited his three Eumenides in paint', Sinclair has written, referring to *Three Studies for Figures at the Base of a Crufixion* 1944 with its gruesome and distorted creatures which Bacon identified as the Furies of the Oresteia myth.[35] But some art historians have cautioned against such moral and biographical interpretations. Mark Roskill, comparing Bacon to the sixteenth-century Mannerists, writes that 'If both Rosso Fiorentino's art and Bacon's look "sick" to us, this is because they play upon our sensations in parallel ways, not because their periods gave them the relevant imagery and mood'.[36]

In interviews, Bacon would insist on artistic reasons for choices of form or image. Pressed on why one of the figures in *Crucifixion* 1965 wears a swastika arm-band, he disconcertingly replied that he wanted to 'break the continuity of the arm and to add the colour ... You may say it was a stupid thing to do, but it was done entirely as part of trying to make the figure work ... formally.'[37] But if Bacon was a formalist, his was a deliberate inversion – perversion even – of formalism. Roger Fry could admire the downward movement of mass in a crucifixion; Bacon went further in blasphemous misreading, claiming that upside down a Cimabue Crucifixion reminded him of 'a worm crawling down the cross.'[38]

Just as the Mannerists subverted the classical perfection of Raphael, so Bacon took from artists of calm and measure – the unaffected naturalist Velázquez, the cool classicist Ingres, the rationalist pioneer photographer Eadweard Muybridge – twisting and turning their images around for his own expressive purpose. Velázquez's portrait of Pope Innocent X became his screaming, caged popes; Ingres's idealised Oedipus became a bloody-bandaged athlete; Muybridge's male wrestlers, naked for the purpose of documenting movement, metamorphosed into male lovers. Such deconstruction was never idle parody, however: for he was attracted to his sources precisely because they achieve the heightened reality he was after in his own work.

'Illustration' was the cat Bacon wished to lose while keeping its grin. He sought a radical dissociation between brushstrokes and the forms they seek to denote, and yet he was disdainful of abstraction, of allowing disengaged marks to slip into mere decoration. He had to hold the tension between gesture and appearance; his whole art, in other words, was a wager on the duality of form and content. He was a compulsive gambler; unlike Freud, who actually liked losing money, Bacon had to win. Similarly, he 'played' at painting until the right accident came along. 'I want a very ordered image, but I want it to come about by chance', he said.[39]

It is because he wanted 'to distort the thing far beyond the appearance, but in the distortion to bring it back to a recording of the appearance' that he preferred to work from photographs for his portraits, the lion's share of his œuvre.[40] He was served by battered photos of such 'sitters' as Lucian Freud, George Dyer, and Isabel Rawsthorne taken by John Deakin, partly because he was more interested in recording memories of appearances than in achieving formal likenesses, but also because he acknowledged that most people would view what he did to their features as 'injury', and their discomfort would inhibit him.

Bacon wanted to show the body as spasm, the face as flesh, but once initial shock at the gruesomeness of flesh rendered as meat and viscera spewed outwards is registered, the ongoing violence comes down as much to alertness and will to life as it does to proximity to danger or death. The pronounced awkwardness of his cross-legged seated men betokens alert passivity (a similar state to Moore's reclining women). As for danger, according to Georges Bataille, whose journal *Documents* [41] Bacon devoured in the 1930s: 'Only when death is at stake does life seem to reach the extreme incandescence of light'.

FAMILY ROMANCE is the psychoanalytic term for a child's fantasy of noble ancestry in contrast to the humdrum parentage allotted him. For Lucian Freud, however, the syndrome was reversed, as the aura of his grandfather was projected upon him by his peers. During the War, while still a teenager, he published drawings in *Horizon*, the house journal of advanced culture in Britain. Child-like, psychologically intense, and strangely fey, these related to the prevailing elegiac, introverted style in British art, Neo-Romanticism, although Freud later professed a 'horror of the idyllic'.[42] Still lifes bringing together such disparate elements as a stuffed zebra's head, a tulip stem, paper bags and a piece of fruit had surrealist charge (no. 10), bringing art history full circle, as the Surrealists themselves had taken their cue from Sigmund Freud.

Bored though he must be by the comparisons, Freud actually gets closer, in the way he paints, to the trappings of psychoanalysis. Like analysis, painting must take place in familiar rooms.[43] Sitters often recline on a couch, an old chesterfield whose stuffing protrudes from various wounds. Between every stroke, the painter cleans his brush on a rag, the painting equivalent of the notorious pregnant pauses of the talking cure. Both painter and psychoanalyst have broken with taboo in subjecting their own daughter(s) to their particular mode of analysis.[44]

Despite Freud's intense realism and his commitment to working from life, an element of - theatre seeps from his lifestyle into his canvases. To writer Marina Warner, Freud is 'a defining

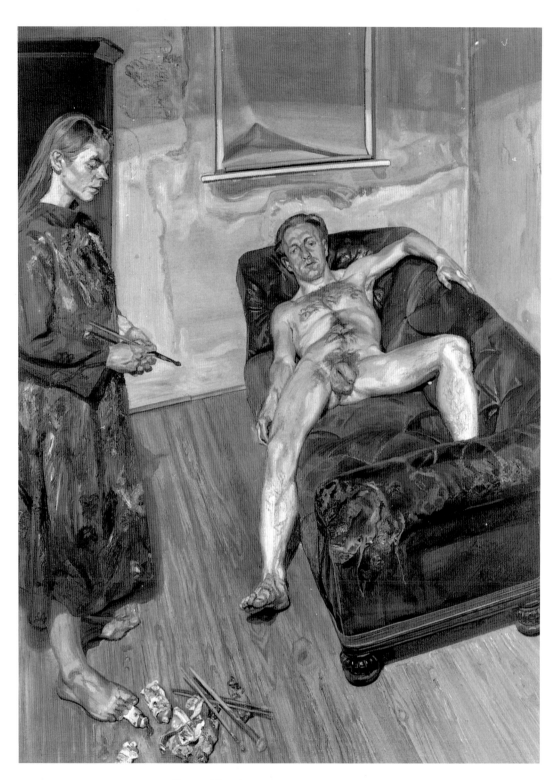

Lucian Freud *Painter and Model* 1986–87
Astrup Fearnley Collection

anti-hero' who might have been invented by Musil or Proust, not just because he is 'a kind of slumming Faust who prowls low-life pubs and eats woodcock for breakfast', but because, ensconced in his studio, he addresses a fundamental existential concern, 'the attraction and repulsion of the flesh'.[45] It is in his depiction of flesh that Freud's painterly concerns and symbolic relationship to the world become enmeshed. John Richardson has asked, 'Isn't the potential of paint to *become* flesh and not merely to simulate it what all Freud's late works celebrate?'[46] Freud himself has said: 'I want my paint to WORK AS FLESH.'[47]

Both Bacon and Freud recall De Kooning's remark that flesh was the reason oil paint was invented. Writing of Bacon in 1957 David Sylvester remarked on the expressive fluidity of 'paint that brings flesh into being and at the same time dissolves it'.[48] Bacon combined oil and acrylic on the same canvas such that the organic-based medium is reserved for the human part to contrast with the inanimate background which is in plastic-based acrylic. Bacon's example made Freud realise the limitations of his flat, linear early style. 'I hoped that if I concentrated enough, the intensity of scrutiny alone would force life into the pictures', he had thought,[49] but he came to realise that volume was essential too. In the 1960s he changed from sable brushes to the much coarser hog's hair brush, started to use leaded paints, and abandoned the polished look of Northern Renaissance painting for expressive, encrusted surfaces.

In certain pictures, 'paint as flesh' is almost played out as an allegory. *Painter and Model* 1986–87 has a naked man reclining on the chesterfield, his whole body open and exposed, while to his right, a woman in a paint-spattered dress holds a brush in her hands.[50] Paint-tubes and brushes are at her feet; green paint issues from one tube pressed under her toe; the staining on her body recalls the accumulated patches to be found on Freud's studio walls, depicted in other canvases. The symbolism is almost lurid as the model is besmirched with paint and discharges paint.

One of his paintings of Leigh Bowery focuses entirely on the performer's genitals. It has been described as a pendant to Courbet's *L'Origine du Monde* (Freud has also depicted women's spread thighs) but bearing in mind Renoir's claim to have painted with his penis it could equally be read as an extension of the paint-flesh equation. Freud once had a cast of Rodin's *Balzac* in his entrance hall, a portrait in which priapism is a metaphor for creative drive.

Freud prefers to paint people he knows, ideally people who are close to him. He is more interested in what is going on in people's heads, he claims, than in the way their bodies reflect light. This may seem a curious claim when usually his sitters wear a nonchalant, resigned, neutral expression. But the great achievement of Freud is to paint flesh with an intensity as if he were painting a face, in contrast to Bacon, who tried to paint the face as if it were just flesh. Sometimes, as if to reverse Magritte's *Rape* of 1934, where a woman's face is transposed with her sexual anatomy, the stretched torsos of Freud's supine women seem to take on facial features. The flesh is truly charged with personality.

UNLIKE BACON and Freud, Frank Auerbach does not frequent casinos or turf accountants yet he defines art like a gambler: 'a means of combating despair', 'catching a fleeting moment', 'playing a small trick with time.' Painting involves high stakes, literally hundreds of failed attempts before pulling off the 'trick' he is after. Extravagant heaps of expensive oils and immeasurable sweat are invested in 'shots' statistically unlikely to yield a win.

There is is no polite Proustian reverie about Auerbach's 'small trick with time'; it goes to the heart of his identity as a survivor of the Holocaust, which claimed his family, and as an artist who formed his language under the shadow of the Bomb. Auerbach himself believes that great art is always autobiographical: Picasso would not have made his breakthrough discoveries had he not painted *Les Demoiselles d'Avignon* tormented by the prospect of syphilis.[51]

There is an atmosphere of nuclear fission in Auerbach's paintings of the 1950s: inscrutable depictions of the people closest to him, or of demolition sites and meat markets, achieved either in dark, murky hues or pigment so virulent as to offend the eye. Paintings of this period were obsessively built up. Accretions generated mystique, if not illegibility. To John Berger, they 'looked as if they had been painted in the dark with a candle and a stick'.[52] For David Sylvester – who welcomed Auerbach's debut as the most significant since Bacon's – they involved 'a sensation curiously like that of running our fingertips over the contours of a head near us in the dark, reassured by its presence, disturbed by its otherness, doubting what it is, and then whether it is.'[53]

Clarity was enhanced when Auerbach switched from adding and adding, until he got what he was after, to scraping down after each unsuccessful session. Now the typical mood in an Auerbach is of bravura and joy. There is still the leaning towards the haptic detected by Sylvester, but the sense of reliefs carved in paint has given way to the sense of spontaneous eruptions of gesture and colour. Sheer physicality constantly brings to mind the image's moment of becoming; the oil paint is so thick and luscious it can look as if it has not yet dried. Works by Auerbach and Kossoff can indeed take years to dry.

'He needed one hundred sessions of work for one still life, one hundred and fifty sittings for a portrait. What we call his work was for him only a series of attempts towards the completed work.'[54] This is the opening sentence of Merleau-Ponty's essay on Cézanne. By Auerbach's own admission, a painted portrait can take one hundred to one hundred and fifty attempts to get right; a charcoal drawing can be as arduous. Some sitters have taken photographs after each session before the scraping down or rubbing away took place. A sequence of such photographs by the late Sandra Fisher, Kitaj's wife, was reproduced in his 1978 Hayward Gallery catalogue.[55] Many of these 'failures' look to be quite presentable Auerbachs. They reinforce how subjective completeness and success are for the artist, but they also attest to how overriding is his concern with truth. He is not content simply to produce a fine image. He could after all have kept the near misses and begun again on a fresh canvas or page.

Frank Auerbach's is a paradoxical project: works of a hard-won status are in the final analysis painterly convulsions; a miraculous coming together of chance effects is underwritten by rigorous classical structure; objects that are blatantly autonomous are mortgaged to the process by which they come about.

For all the obsessive re-working and the insistence on the presence of the sitter, the resemblance between the pulverised conglomeration of paint and the person it represents ultimately rests not just on the artist's empathy with his subject but on an element of caricature: the recurring features of regular sitters are as basic as a jutting jaw, a prominent forehead, or small, dark eyes. It begs the question: Why does the sitter have to be there? For the amount of purely visual information he requires, could he not make do with a photograph, like Bacon? The answer, perhaps, is ethical, in a similar way that Bacon's reason for *not* painting in front of the sitter was ethical. Instead of keeping his friends from the violence he would be doing to them in rendering them as form, Auerbach needs their presence in order to prevent the painting's content declining into an I–It relationship, in order to infuse emotional, humane, life-giving I–Thou force to the paint.

IN A RARE and extraordinarily poignant statement, Leon Kossoff wrote: 'I was born in a now demolished building in City Road not far from St Paul's … Ever since the age of twelve, I have drawn and painted London … The strange ever-changing light, the endless streets and the shuddering feel of the sprawling city linger in my mind like a faintly glimmering memory of a long-forgotten, perhaps never experienced childhood, which, if rediscovered and illuminated, would ameliorate the pain of the present.'[56] John Russell has suggested that 'although no two people could outwardly have less in common, there is something of Proust' in these sentiments.[57]

Francis Bacon, with typical existentialist panache, liked to boast of his 'exhilarated despair'. The equivalent oxymoronic tag for Kossoff could be 'elated melancholy'. His colours are muted (murky in the early pictures), earthy browns and greens, steely blues and greys. His scenery is understated, suburban. His people look resigned to their private miseries. Yet the swirling paint and bursting design invariably sing like the cathartic climax of a minor-key adagio by Mahler or Sibelius.

Kossoff's attitude towards the social environment seems very different from the other painters. This in turn reflects the contrasting personal circumstances of a man who preferred family life to the Soho scene. He avidly treads the streets of London, but not as a *flâneur*. Bacon defined the city as a sexual gymnasium; for Kossoff it is the repository of primary associations. Where Bacon, Freud and Kitaj depict neutral, anonymous interiors, Kossoff portrays specific sites imbued with their history and character. The least given to overt symbolism of any of the School, he nonetheless chooses buildings – landmarks from his childhood, demolition sites, buildings associated with children such as swimming-pools or schools – of special resonance.

Andrews and Auerbach have made paintings after specific places – Ayers Rock and Primrose Hill – but Kossoff is the most topographical of the artists. He draws doggedly *in situ* the places he intends to paint; he has to draw a new model hundreds of times over a period of at least a year before he can paint her. It is intensely important for him to know his subject through seeing. Yet ironically all this specific information must be purged if the image is to work in paint. 'I have never finished a picture without first experiencing a huge emptying of all factual and topographical knowledge', he has written. He has also spoken of trying to make paintings more like the sitter, 'more real, more intense', but then being overtaken by something: 'I stop thinking, for better or worse.'[58]

This combination of topography and 'expressionism' is found in other artists – Jack Butler Yeats, Oskar Kokoschka. To the late Peter Fuller, however, Kossoff embodied, simultaneously, the most contradictory aspects of Jackson Pollock, the American action painter, and William Coldstream, the British realist, while escaping their respective failures: 'he is neither subsumed and lost within his boundless self; nor is he saddled with an arid and "untranscendable" set of historically specific representational devices'.[59]

Peter Fuller was an outspoken critic of institutionalised avant-gardism and a staunch defender of what he saw as painting that extends the grand tradition. Kossoff, who at the time of writing this Fuller believed to be the greatest living British painter, was an inspiration to his critical concept, 'redemption through form'. He identified the impetus to combine fastidious realism and expressive spontaneity in the person of David Bomberg, whose class at the Borough Polytechnic Kossoff and Auerbach attended together. Bomberg exhorted his students to look beyond the life-room for their subject. A charismatic teacher, one of his *bons mots* was 'seek the spirit in the mass', a phrase that reverberates in the paintings of Auerbach and Kossoff as well as in the writings of Fuller.[60]

The similarities between Auerbach and Kossoff, who were once close friends, are undeniable, but have been exaggerated. Helen Lessore has usefully compared their situation to 'that of two brothers who appear to strangers as having a strong resemblance, while inside the family and among close friends their difference seems greater than any likeness'.[61] Drawing is important for Auerbach in a different way than for Kossoff: in fact, it is simply another way of making images, and is never preparatory. For Kossoff it is an essential prerequisite. For Auerbach, the sense of structure, in whatever medium, is enhanced by line: his zigzags are never as rushed-off as they appear. Kossoff, on the other hand, literally draws with the brush. In Auerbach, the image is made of paint; in Kossoff it is excavated, by drawing, *from* the paint. The slightly quirky, fish-eye perspective found in Freud is far more intense in Kossoff: figures, buildings, cars look as if they are going to topple under the sheer weight of the pigment or charcoal from which they are made. His Gestalt is so packed-in it seems to pulsate. An expression of Auerbach's actually has greater application to Kossoff: 'vision pushed to its extreme'.[62]

To some, Michael Andrews will seem a fringe member of the School of London. His subjects are predominantly rural, his style remote from 'expressionism'. But his ambitions and anxieties identify him with his friends. His works shed light on theirs.

When Andrews was a star pupil of William Coldstream at the Slade in the early 1950s,[63] he was deeply affected by the writings of Kierkegaard and the new work of Bacon and Giacometti. Euston Road realism and existentialism, like topography and 'expressionism' for Kossoff, were coordinates of a dichotomy which charged his work. For all that Coldstream's reticent, obsessive measuring and recording is seared through with doubt, Coldstream was a painter who fervently aspired to objective realism (see illustration p. 20), whereas Andrews has always been acutely aware of the phenomenological complexities of visual language. Even in his empirical, life-size family portraits of the early 1960s there is, as Peter Fuller noticed, 'clipped *angst* and trim unease'. 'He was temperamentally incapable of expressionism; and yet, equally, he was unable to rest content with the world of appearances'.[64]

The personality of the artist is omnipresent in School of London painting, whether through regular and dramatic self-depiction (Bacon, Freud, Kitaj) or through gestural expressiveness. In Andrews, however, the relative coolness and neutrality of paint application suggests detachment. Although he has done self-portraits, the diminution of selfhood is actually one of his central themes.

Early works depicted disturbing existential unease with the body. *A Man Who Suddenly Fell Over* 1952 catches a middle-aged conventionally dressed man in the moment of suspended crisis; Jonathan Raban has characterised it as 'an upsetting work in every sense of the word' in which 'your own dimensions and disposition in space are called into question: what are you doing here? and where is here?'.[65] The 'party paintings' of the 1960s explore the complexities of image projection in a forced, social environment. Out of this conception of the face as mask came elaborate distortions of physiognomy; like Sickert, Andrews was fascinated by newspaper photographs of celebrities. They have an unexpected quirkiness which reveals an alienation from the subject's self-image. He comes very close to Kitaj and to Richard Hamilton (see illustration p. 20) in the stretched, twisted and compressed faces in *Good and Bad at Games*, a triptych of 1964–68.

Andrews developed the theme of ego-abnegation when, either in R. D. Laing or Alan Watts (cult writers of the 1960s)[66] he encountered the term 'skin-encapsulated ego'.[67] At the same time, he saw a newspaper photograph of a hot-air balloon floating over Gloucestershire. Together, these triggered a series of eerily serene unpeopled landscapes featuring the balloon as a metaphor for selfhood (no. 37). The exquisite Whistlerian nocturne of a black balloon over Waterloo Bridge, even more than his other Thames pictures, forms an inadvertent pendant to Kitaj's pastoral depiction of the River Thames (*Tempesta* 1992–93).

The *Lights* series (nos. 37–39) represented the culmination of a certain line of thought in Andrews's paintings, starting with radical challenges to the notion of self and ending with an almost oceanic conception of its evaporation. It is no surprise that after the balloon itself made its departure he did his most hermetically sealed, expressionless, and ethereal works to date, his series of coastlines. In these and other recent works by Andrews, awkwardness gives way to seeming straightforwardness as a means of disconcerting the viewer.

Andrews spent the best part of the 1980s painting Ayers Rock and other geological formations in Central Australia (nos. 40, 41). Intending to visit the rock in 1968, he finally got there in 1983, climbing it several times and drawing it. Inspired by the religious attitude of Aborigines towards what they call Uluru, Andrews titled his exhibition of the series *Rock of Ages Cleft for Me* after a hymn remembered from his Methodist childhood, the second line of which, 'Let me hide myself in Thee', is the true source of its appeal to him. The paintings were made in his Norfolk studio and based as much on tourist-board photos as on his own drawings. The resulting images reflect a sense of otherness, distance, and mystery. There are strange and unexpected resonances between Andrews's 'cathedral' – as the largest rock formation is known – and Leon Kossoff's depiction of Christchurch, Spitalfields (nos. 30, 31). Both Ayers Rock and Christchurch are weirdly incongruous monumental presences, the one in a desert as flat as Andrews's native Norfolk, the other in the huddled East End streets of Kossoff's childhood. Each artist has found a potent symbol of remote archetypal longing in a 'gross material fact' of overwhelming actuality.

No visitor to R. B. Kitaj's first solo exhibition in 1963 could have predicted that one day he would belong in what is seen as a counter-modernist school of figurative or realist painters.[68] The hallmark of this show, entitled *Pictures with Commentary, Pictures without Commentary*, was its intellectualism. Explicatory texts, philosophical references and literary *bons mots* appeared on or besides the canvases. Appropriation and fragmentation took their cue from Surrealism, cinema, T. S. Eliot and Ezra Pound, and the iconology of Aby Warburg. 'For me, books are what trees are for the landscape painter,' Kitaj has said.[69] He has never lost the ambition to address big themes and ideological concerns in art.

That in 1964 Michael Andrews and Victor Willing should view Kitaj as a conceptual artist *avant la lettre* is a measure of his perceived distance from future colleagues. 'The thing I like about Kitaj', Andrews said, 'is that he seems to have his own house in order, and that the emotion of the pictures is about ideas and things outside himself, and not about his frame of mind.'[70]

It is now clear that Kitaj's rampant, quirky intellectualism is very much a product of temperament, of a restless, agitated mind. Un-at homeness is both Kitaj's theme and style. Where Bacon or Auerbach set out to find the painterly language which can assume the burden of their alienations, Kitaj's alienation is from expression itself. His personal artistic renewals and impassioned art-world advocacies dramatise a paradoxical state of wanting to belong and wanting to be elsewhere. Thanks to his sense of humour and artistic talent, his malaise becomes, for the viewer, an adventure.

Kitaj's art has undergone radical transformations and reinventions. Where once collaged book covers were enough to trigger associations, he now sets out to create in paint characters as life-like as those in Dickens or Dostoevsky.[71] But his recent retrospective demonstrated the dynamic unity of his multilayered œuvre, which cumulatively reads like a great novel, oscillating between fragmentation and wholeness, montage and narrative, frankness and ambiguity, tragedy and comedy.[72] And like a great novel, the central character, lurching from crisis to crisis, is all the more credible for the fact that he grows.

Already by 1966 Kitaj the Pop Artist showed signs of unrest, delivering fiercely polemical lectures which indicted an international avant-garde remote from human moral concerns. Harshest criticism was reserved for his own work, while significantly, Balthus – the post-surrealist realist – was singled out for praise. Kitaj's personal journey towards a new humanism was temporarily arrested, but ultimately propelled, by a personal tragedy, the suicide of his first wife. Production was halted for several years, but he worked himself back into art by drawing from life. Perhaps witnessing the effects of confusion on the mind of a loved one dampened enthusiasm for fragmentations, although his great paintings of fragments, *The Autumn of Central Paris (After Walter Benjamin)* 1972–73 and *If Not, Not* (no. 61) did come later. But from the 1970s a previously unknown wholeness entered Kitaj's work, in the form of pictures centred on single figures. Encouraged by his new partner Sandra Fisher (whom he married in 1983) and the personal discovery of Degas, he began to use pastels. A new and frank eroticism entered his work.

At the same time as this artistic renewal – rejoining a great tradition and finding community with other artists through it – Kitaj experienced a burgeoning sense of his own Jewishness. An impression of the prodigal son returned to the fold of life-drawing and religious observance would be wide of the mark, however, for Kitaj's researches in Jewish history, his obsession with the Holocaust, and above all his ambition to encapsulate the Kafkaesque experience of Diaspora (un-at homeness, malaise) in art, led away from the dignified, homogeneous, sensual realism of the 1970s pastels to the spatial complexities, bodily and physiognomic distortions and agitated, uncomfortable painterliness of the work of the 1980s and 1990s, periods of major achievement.

Personal crisis again precipitated Kitaj's most recent stylistic departure: first a heart attack and related depression in 1989, then soon after the Tate Gallery's offer to mount a retrospective. These events galvanised Kitaj's existential fear of death and his desire to cheat it by leaving behind significant art after him. Perversely for such a driven artist, he has spoken of wanting to retire, but with one last *putsch*. Candidly and calculatedly, he embarked upon his 'old-age' style, in emulation of such art heroes as Michelangelo, Titian, Degas, and Picasso. Richard Wollheim justly questions whether there is really such a thing as old-age style, and if a fit man in his late fifties can elect to enter it, but concedes that in the more recent paintings 'Kitaj has painted something that looks "late": that is a fusion of pictorial concerns, purchased at the price – a price that a number of very old and very great painters seemed prepared to pay – of inelegance, of moodiness, even of a certain peremptoriness'.[73] This manifests in Kitaj's robust, awkward drawing, the unmodern (and un-Kitaj) subservience of colour to line, and the scarred exposure of the work's evolution.

FREUD HAS ALSO entered a late style, but in contrast to Kitaj, he got there through 'a long, cautious, courageous haul over tempting Baconian shortcuts', as John Richardson puts it.[74] The paintings of Andrews, Auerbach and Kossoff seem to progress towards clarity, gaiety even, towards 'mature' rather than 'late' style. Bacon's genius, which as Richardson implies is to be envied rather than emulated, was to start with a late style – pungent, urgent, raw but masterful.

In a way, though, all the artists of the School of London are 'late' in their acute consciousness of the unfinished business of the great tradition to which they belong. There is something poignant in the fact that the painting of Freud's which more than any other declared a leap forward in his most recent retrospective was a naked full-length self-portrait (1993). In painterly terms, all six artists in this exhibition stand before their audience exposed, hiding nothing of their identity, qualities, vulnerabilities. Their 'naked ambition' is to paint at the end of this century with the tenacity, intensity and bravura of any other time.

Notes and References

1 The title of this essay is taken from Frank Auerbach's foreword to *Late Sickert* [exhibition catalogue] Arts Council of Great Britain, London, 1982, p.7.

2 To David Mellor in the latter's essay 'Existentialism and Post-War British Art', in Frances Morris (ed.) *Paris Post War: Art and Existentialism 1945–55* [exhibition catalogue] Tate Gallery, London, 1993, p.53.

3 The picture within the picture is *Interior, Vincent Terrace* 1982–84, and the photo within the photo is of Lucian Freud's then recently completed *Large Interior WII (After Watteau)* 1981–83.

4 A fiercely contested and problematic term, 'School of London' has nonetheless a broad currency. After Kitaj, the phrase was used by the painter and art historian Lawrence Gowing (author of the definitive monograph on Freud) to describe a group of artists who 'spend most of their time painting figures, one way or another.' His list, in addition to the six artists exhibited here, included Peter Blake, Jeffrey Camp, Patrick Caulfield, Patrick George, David Hockney, Howard Hodgkin, Allen Jones and Euan Uglow ['Painters of Fact and Feeling' *Sunday Times* 26 October 1980]. 'School of London' was then used for a section of a survey exhibition at the Royal Academy, *British Art in the Twentieth Century*, in 1987, which included Andrews, Auerbach, Bacon, Freud, and Kossoff. Kitaj was included in a different section (with Howard Hodgkin and Malcolm Morley); in the same year Michael Peppiat organised *A School of London: Six Figurative Painters* for the British Council, with the same cast as the present exhibition. *The School of London* was the title of a book by Alistair Hicks (London, 1989) on the resurgence of figurative painting, including younger artists inspired by the lead of the first generation. Members of the original group (minus Kitaj) have featured in several exhibitions concerned with realism (eg. *Eight Figurative Painters*, Yale Center for British Art, 1981; *The Pursuit of the Real*, Manchester and London, 1990; *Transformations of Experience*, Sainsbury Centre for the Visual Arts, Norwich, 1991).

5 Michael Andrews was elected a member of this prestigious establishment in 1993 but resigned in 1994; R. B. Kitaj has been an RA since 1985.

6 Freud was the subject of many portraits by Bacon. Bacon also painted Auerbach, while both in turn sat

for Freud, who has also painted Michael Andrews with his wife. Kitaj has incorporated portraits of Auerbach and Bacon in his works, and was himself the subject of an etching by Auerbach, as were Kossoff and Freud. Michael Andrews's group portrait of the Colony Room private drinking club in Soho includes Freud and Bacon. Freud purchased *Two Figures* 1953, an important work by Bacon. Kitaj has an extensive and important collection of his friends' works.

7 *The Human Clay: an exhibition selected by R. B. Kitaj*, Arts Council of Great Britain, London, 1976, p.7. The title *The Human Clay* comes from 'Letter to Lord Byron', a poem by W. H. Auden: 'To me Art's subject is the human clay'.

8 The director of the Beaux Arts Gallery in London and mother of the painter John Lessore, Helen Lessore was a significant painter in her own right. See also note 19.

9 David Sylvester *Interviews with Francis Bacon* London, 1975, pp.59–60.

10 *The Listener* 16 January 1958.

11 *The Artist's Eye, an exhibition selected by R. B. Kitaj* [exhibition catalogue] National Gallery, London, 1980. Alex Haley is the African-American author of *Roots*. Bacon and Freud were also selectors of 'Artist's Eye' exhibitions at the National Gallery in 1985 and 1987 respectively.

12 See R. B. Kitaj *First Diasporist Manifesto* London, 1989.

13 *Michael Andrews* [exhibition catalogue] Arts Council of Great Britain, 1981, introduction by Lawrence Gowing, p.12.

14 R. D. Laing, whose seminal text *The Divided Self* (1960) was a great influence on Michael Andrews, is one writer to compare Beckett and Bacon: '[In Beckett] there is a contradictory sense of self in its "health and validity" to mitigate the despair, terror and boredom of existence. In painting, Francis Bacon, among others, seems to be dealing with similar issues'. Quoted from Keith Patrick's introduction to *From Bacon to Now: The Outsider in British Figuration*, [exhibition catalogue] Palazzo Vecchio, Florence, 1991, a survey exhibition of nineteen artists which included Auerbach, Bacon, Freud, Kitaj, and Kossoff.

15 Herbert Read *Contemporary British Art* (second edition) Harmondsworth, 1964, p.35.

16 Quoted from Mel Gooding 'The Phenomenon of Presence: The Paintings of Frank Auerbach' in *Frank Auerbach: Recent Work* [exhibition catalogue] Rijksmuseum Vincent van Gogh, Amsterdam, 1989, p.3.

17 For example, Victor Willing, a painter often associated with the School of London, in conversation with Michael Andrews: 'MA: "Existentialism" of one kind or another was a prevalent attitude when we were at the Slade. VW: What we thought was "existentialism"! It gave our endeavours a certain glamour, so we clung to the idea. The Giacometti idea, that sort of life, that sort of painting... ...Sartre's essay on Giacometti is full of the most tremendous rubbish when you come to look at it.' Michael Andrews and Victor Willing 'Morality and the Model' in *Art and Literature* Summer 1964, p.49.

18 The leading members of this group, which exhibited together at the 1956 Venice Biennale, were John Bratby, Derrick Greaves, Edward Middleditch and Jack Smith.

19 Andrews, Auerbach, Bacon and Kossoff all exhibited there. Together with Freud, who had been due to show with her but was taken up by another dealer, each artist is the subject of a chapter in Lessore's book, *A Partial Testament: Essays on Some Moderns in the Great Tradition* (London, 1986). Other chapters are devoted to Cézanne, Giacometti, Aitchison, Balthus, Lundquist, Mason, and Uglow.

20 'Idealism' in *Art News* 12 May 1910; quoted from Osbert Sitwell (ed.) *A Free House, or The Artist as Craftsman: being the writings of Walter Richard Sickert* London, 1947, p.208.

21 Claude Rogers founded a short-lived art school on Euston Road in 1937 to employ artists during the Depression. The term continued to be applied to a somewhat dour brand of realism itself indebted to the Camden Town Group from earlier in the century of which Sickert was a member. William Coldstream, discussed below in connection with his pupil Michael Andrews, and Lawrence Gowing, quoted in several places in this essay, were both associated with Euston Road.

22 Michel Leiris *Francis Bacon* London, 1987, p.6.

23 'The American Action Painters' in *Art News* December 1952, p.22.

24 *Metamorphosis* 1952 and *Together* 1955, the latter with Eduardo Paolozzi. Mazzetti is the subject of an important painting by Andrews, *Lorenza Mazzetti in Italy*, of 1954.

25 Kitaj in Richard Morphet (ed.) *R. B. Kitaj: A Retrospective* [exhibition catalogue] Tate Gallery, London, 1994, p.158.

26 Bowery died in January 1995 aged 33.

27 Vol ii, no iii; reprinted in *The Independent* 11 January 1992. Bruce Bernard's colour photograph appeared on the cover of the Saturday magazine section.

28 Catherine Lampert has detected 'the same turn of the head and the excitement of cloth against and near skin which argues for discovering beauty in oddness rather than in an ideal'. *Lucian Freud: Recent Work* [exhibition catalogue] Whitechapel Art Gallery, London, 1993, p.25.

29 Translation by Anthony Rudolf, Menard Press, London, 1988, p.16.

30 *R. B. Kitaj: A Retrospective op.cit.* p.221.

31 David Sylvester *Looking at Giacometti* London, 1994, p.18. The chapter from which this quotation is taken was part of a monograph written by Sylvester in 1959 and withdrawn from the publisher because of the author's 'doubt'. Frank Auerbach tells me that he read a draft of the monograph at the time.

32 Kitaj most likely read Maurice Merleau-Ponty's classic 1946 essay 'Cézanne's Doubt' translated and published in *Partisan Review* that year. (He collected old copies of this journal, which was the subject of an image in his series *In Our Time*; see note 71). Incidentally, Cézanne is an 'outsider' par excellence. The hero of Camus's novel *L'étranger* comes to mind on reading Merleau-Ponty's observation that 'He painted on the afternoon his mother died'.

33 *Michael Andrews op.cit.* p.24.

34 *Interviews with Francis Bacon op.cit.* p.65.

35 Andrew Sinclair *Francis Bacon: His Life and Violent Times* London, 1993, p.96.

36 Mark Roskill 'Francis Bacon as a Mannerist' in *Art International* September 1963, p.44.

37 *Interviews with Francis Bacon op.cit.* p.65.

38 *ibid.* p.14. The figure derived from Cimabue is to be found in the right-hand panel of *Three Studies for a Crucifixion* 1962.

39 *ibid.* p.56.

40 *ibid.* p.40.

41 See Dawn Ades 'A Web of Images' in *Francis Bacon* [exhibition catalogue] Tate Gallery, London, 1985 for a detailed discussion of Bacon's borrowings from this and other avant-garde journals.

42 Quoted from John Richardson 'Paint Becomes Flesh' in *The New Yorker* 13 December 1993.

43 Freud lived in the seedy neighbourhood of Paddington from the 1940s, and moved to Holland Park in the late 1970s.

44 Sigmund Freud undertook the training analysis of his daughter Anna (Lucian's aunt) to protect family secrets from colleagues; Lucian Freud has painted many nude portraits of several of his daughters.

45 Marina Warner 'The Unblinking Eye' in *The New York Times Magazine* 4 December 1988.

46 Richardson *op.cit.*

47 Lawrence Gowing *Lucian Freud* London, 1982, quoted in Richardson *ibid.*

48 David Sylvester 'In Camera' in *Encounter* April 1957, p.24.

49 Robert Hughes *Lucian Freud: Paintings* [exhibition catalogue] British Council, London, 1987, p.14.

50 The woman is the painter Celia Paul who is also the model for *Naked Girl with Egg* 1980–81 (no.19).

51 The artist in conversation with the author, 1990. cf also: 'I feel Titian's themes stand in some sort of way for events in his life. Far too little attention has been paid to the fact that in the convincing pictures of mythological and biblical themes the people are very probably portraits, I'm more and more convinced of that.' (Catherine Lampert 'A conversation with Frank Auerbach' in *Frank Auerbach* [exhibition catalogue] Arts Council of Great Britain, London, 1978, p.16.)

52 John Berger 'A Stick in the Dark' in *New Statesman* 28 November 1959.

53 David Sylvester 'Nameless Structures' in *New Statesman* 21 April 1961.

54 Merleau-Ponty, *op.cit.*; the essay also appeared in *Art and Literature* Spring 1965.

55 A montage of 25 of the 27 photographs taken by Jill Phillips for her portrait drawing was reproduced as the frontispiece of this catalogue.

56 Quoted in *Leon Kossoff: Recent Paintings and Drawings* [exhibition catalogue] Fischer Fine Art, London, 1972, p.5.

57 John Russell 'Leon Kossoff' in *The New York Times* 11 March 1983.

58 Quoted in Andrew Graham-Dixon 'When the Sparks Fly' in *The Independent* 16 September 1988.

59 Peter Fuller 'Leon Kossoff' in *Art Monthly* May 1979, p.12.

60 Fuller was pointed in the direction of Bomberg by his one-time mentor John Berger.

61 Helen Lessore *A Partial Testament* London, 1986, p.56.

62 Frank Auerbach 'Fragments from a Conversation' in *X: A Quarterly Review* Vol I no 1 November 1959, p.32. *X* was a short-lived but highly significant literary journal edited by David Wright and Patrick Swift which published texts by Beckett, Bonnefoy, Giacometti, Kokoschka, Masson, Pasternak and Pound; a younger generation of British poets, including Barker, Graves, MacDiarmid, Sisson, and Smith; and younger painters, including Aitchison, Andrews, and Auerbach.

63 Andrews studied at the Slade from 1949–1953; fellow students included Tim Behrens, whose portrait he painted, and Paula Rego, Euan Uglow and Victor Willing, artists who have featured in revisionist accounts of the School of London.

64 Peter Fuller 'Michael Andrews: Recent Paintings' in *The Burlington Magazine* July 1986, p.530.

65 Jonathan Raban *Michael Andrews 'The Delectable Mountain'* [exhibition catalogue] Whitechapel Art Gallery, London, 1991, p.15.

66 R. D. Laing, psychoanalyst and outspoken critic of psychiatry, was the author of *The Divided Self*, *The Politics of Experience*, and other works; Alan Watts wrote on Zen Buddhism, a subject he helped popularize in the West.

67 The French psychoanalyst Didier Anzieu, who has formulated a whole theory around the notion of 'skin ego', has described Francis Bacon as a 'painter of rents in the Skin Ego' (Didier Anzieu *A Skin for Thought: Interviews with Gilbert Tarrab* London, 1990, p.122).

68 This exhibition took place with Marlborough Fine Art, who remain his dealers. This gallery has represented Bacon from 1958 and Auerbach from 1965. Kossoff staged an exhibition at Marlborough in 1966 and has taken part in group exhibitions there, as have Andrews and Freud.

69 Interview in *Time* 1965 quoted from Marco Livingstone *R. B. Kitaj* Oxford, 1985, p.16.

70 'Morality and the Model' *op.cit.* p.62.

71 *In Our Time*, a 1969 series of 50 screenprints, consists simply of blown-up book covers, rarities from the library of a bibliophile ranging from modernist classics to anti-semitic tracts and cheap novellas.

72 *R. B. Kitaj: A Retrospective* Tate Gallery, London; Los Angeles County Museum of Art; Metropolitan Museum of Art, New York; June 1994–May 1995

73 Richard Wollheim 'Kitaj: Recollections and Reflections' in Morphet (ed.) *op.cit.* p.42.

74 Richardson *op.cit.*

Michael Andrews in his Norfolk studio 1990
On the easel: *Portrait of Bruce Bernard* 1990; behind the artist, *A View from Uamh Mhòr* (no.42) in an early state
photo: Bruce Bernard

Painter Friends

BRUCE BERNARD

I HAVE, AND I DO NOT use the word out of only formal deference, had the honour of knowing four of the participants in this exhibition quite well over periods from well over forty years to fifty-two. I met Lucian Freud first in 1943, Francis Bacon very probably in 1948, and Michael Andrews and Frank Auerbach in the early fifties. I cannot claim to know Leon Kossoff at all well, but I briefly attended St Martin's School of Art at the same time, spoke to him a little there, and we have met a few times since. I very much look forward to his Venice Biennale this summer as I am certain that he will prove as worthy of the honour as anyone. Ron Kitaj I know only from a few polite exchanges at art gatherings of various kinds. Although on close friendly terms with two of them, Freud and Andrews, cordial ones with Auerbach and for nearly all the time I knew him with Bacon, I have not always been in close touch with any of them, either because of absence on one side or the other or their natural reclusiveness (apart from Bacon). They have, though – owing to their shared avocation, their very important achievements within it and their very interesting though entirely distinct personalities – always been essential to me to the extent that I can imagine life on earth without their presence less easily than I can the absence of anyone else.

It was while I was at school in 1942 that I first came across Lucian Freud in person, but also Francis Bacon in the form of a reproduction in Herbert Read's *Art Now*. It was his 1933 *Crucifixion*, a spectral standing figure that appeared to be partly fashioned with metal rods glowing in a darkness that seems to promise the illuminated spaces in which he would later on set his dramas of human mortality and futility. It looked quite as strong to me as the Picasso reproduced on the opposite page, however ardent my precocious admiration was for the giant of modernism.

I met Lucian during the school holidays at 23 Clarendon Road w.11, a house occupied by a cashiered officer of the Queen's Own Cameron Highlanders, who was paying attention to my widowed mother, and his two sons and daughter. The eldest son, Nigel, was sophisticated for his years and had engaged the interest of Peter Watson, the rich financier of *Horizon* magazine and

43

Lucian Freud in his studio 1990, with *Leigh Bowery (Seated)* 1990
photo: Bruce Bernard

collector of art. (Peter Watson was probably the best of the homosexual patrons of the arts around at the time and a decent, generous man.) Lucian's talent and no doubt his extraordinary looks and personality had also attracted Watson's friendship and he had become friendly with Nigel. I was very impressed by Lucian's exotic and somewhat demonic aura, and my mother warned me that being Sigmund Freud's grandson he might be dangerous to know – though this of course made me even more interested in him. I saw and was very impressed by his drawings reproduced in *Horizon* and also by one of Nigel which was the first work by a real artist that I had ever felt a personal connection with. In spite of my devotion to Picasso, Braque, Matisse, Rouault and Miró I felt that Lucian's rather idiosyncratic, more naturalistic and Northern view of things came from a powerful artistic personality and it seemed certain to me, as it did to many much older and wiser, that he was definitely going somewhere. I think that he regarded me and my family with only momentary curiosity and remember him calling me 'Bryce' with a soft German 'ʀ'. But he soon disappeared from Clarendon Road, or from my ken at least, as if in a puff of smoke, and I didn't see him again as far as I remember until I observed his fleeting figure on the Rue du Bac in Paris late in 1947 when he said 'Hello Bryce' and disappeared again. I had, though, seen his show at the Lefevre Gallery in Bond Street in 1944 and been quite if not hugely impressed – but I would especially admire the *Dead Heron* 1945 which I saw a little later and which still looks utterly singular and beautiful to me. I also took a keen interest in his *Interior in Paddington* 1951 whose subject was Harry Diamond, now a well-known photographer and a friend I had made in Soho before the picture was painted. It was both a brilliant prize-winning picture and a significant stride for Lucian in every way, and should surely have come in first instead of second in the Festival of Britain competition of 1951, far ahead of William Gear's tame semi-abstraction, which won.

But I didn't really make friends with Lucian until the very early sixties though I saw him from time to time on his forays into Soho, which I had somewhat reluctantly been obliged to regard as my natural habitat, and would continue to do so for an unconscionable time. Sometimes he was with Francis Bacon, but more often, I think, looking to extend his range of female acquaintanceship and to survey the scene while backing horses.

Since then Lucian's career has been extraordinary and his personal life no less so. His avowed determination to do nothing whatever that he doesn't want to can make one wince a little, but it has produced one of the few great bodies of work ever painted in this country. All the lily-livered carping about the inhumanity of his 'naked portraits' which are in fact exactly the opposite in sentiment, is now almost completely silenced. He now seems to have reached something like a 'sunlit upland' in his work, populated, in part at least, by monumentally overweight people who have enjoyed in the most wholesome way their unlooked for 'immortality'. (There is no doubt in my mind that the late Leigh Bowery, however sad his fate, derived a very welcome sustenance from his work for Lucian.) Quite a few of Lucian's daughters write interesting first and even second novels, for which he provides really charming, relaxed dust jackets – and they seem to like him quite a lot. If he has sometimes, or for all I know often, behaved like a shit, as many of the best, and perhaps even more of the worst artists do, then he has left a lot of life and intelligence-enhancing images behind him. And I'm sure that during the years that remain to him he will continue to increase and enrich that legacy, as well as remaining a person for whom many feel more and more appreciation.

Francis Bacon, though he had lived in London throughout the war and exhibited the triptych that established him as an artist at the Lefevre Gallery in 1945, hit Soho like a welcome and highly stimulating whirlwind in 1948. He seemed quite unique to me at twenty – magical – his extraordinary energy and intelligence (which needed no conventional demonstration) allowing him a marvellous overflow of frivolity that came from far too interesting a person to be regarded simply as 'camp'. Lucian, who had known him in London before the end of the war, later described him as being at this time 'the wisest and wildest' person he had ever known. Francis's centre in Soho was Muriel Belcher's Colony Room, a one-room drinking club as singular as its proprietor, and then about seventy-five per cent queer but gradually becoming fifty per cent and more 'straight' (if any members could be so described, or as 'normal' either) and with children (accompanied by their parents) unofficially welcome in the afternoon. I first met Lucian's eldest daughters there when they were about four. Francis and Muriel had a very special love for each other and for a time she paid him £10 a night with drinks to bring people with money in. He had little difficulty in finding them and he was also pursued by those who knew what a remarkable painter he was. He could, though, be coldly dismissive and really funnily and mercilessly bitchy when he wasn't seeming actually to radiate sweetness and light. He had no trace whatever of social snobbery, though he was, he said, stimulated in a sexual kind of way by the very rich. But money for him was an imperative fuel of which, at this time and from then on he made sure that any shortage was only very temporary, and in the late forties this was a liberating thought, even vicariously.

I remember being a little disappointed by his first show at the Hanover Gallery in 1949. *Head VI* (often referred to as his first 'screaming Pope'), which can be seen in this exhibition (no. 2), was

Francis Bacon in his studio 1984
photo: Bruce Bernard

in it, and the powerful *Head II* of 1949, but I thought that there was nothing there to compare with the masterpiece *Painting* 1946, shown at the Redfern Gallery the year it was painted. Then quite soon came the actually shocking great painting *Two Figures* 1953, which Erica Brausen of the Hanover had to put in the upstairs gallery in case anyone complained to the police as it turned a photograph by Muybridge (and possibly an indecent snapshot) into a clear suggestion of buggery and also it seemed, though perhaps not everyone saw it that way, the futility of sexual coupling. Not long afterwards, at the Colony, I asked him (I could think of nothing else to say) what he was up to. With a rather wistful smile he said '… well, I'm trying to do something based on Van Gogh but I don't know whether it will work …' and only a few days later Erica asked me to help carry a very wet canvas into her gallery which was one of the series based on Vincent's *The Painter on his Way to Work*. Perhaps only two of them were really fit to enter the canon but the whole idea was so audacious, and one would have thought anyone else unhinged or simply stupid to have attempted it.

Around this time, also in the Colony, I heard someone else, from the City it seemed, asking Francis in a concerned City baritone what he was working on. 'Well' he said rather loudly, in a marvellously ridiculous parody of an artist being interviewed about his work in progress, 'I'm doing a new series of Crucifixions. They're all based on *My Fair Lady* and she's got a green parasol'. It was appallingly funny and it seems very likely that he was alluding to his recent portrait of Cecil Beaton from life which had so horrified its subject that Francis had kindly destroyed it.

Naturally I followed Francis's work to the end and if I liked very little of what came out of his last decade it was because he seemed to have almost entirely displaced his initial inspired exploitation of chance with preconception and virtuosity (a very drawn out process with many powerful syntheses along the way) and his raw-nerved and *real* figures with voluptuous ones or things he only took a curious pleasure in. I very much regret that I fell out with him about a publication idea, because it robbed me of the encouragement his friendship gave me. His rejection of Frank's mature works and most of Lucian's, and in the end their friendship, had already been painful, and it was dispiriting when he seemed to have become interested in *accumulating* money. But he was still never less than very generous, and it was more than depressing for me, on the last two occasions that we met, to share a bottle of cold, newly opened claret with him costing £90 or more when he didn't much want it himself and certainly not in my company.

I wish that he could have died laughing at a really funny and entirely new notion. I will never forget what exhilarating company he could be, or my conviction that his greatness as a twentieth-century artist will be acknowledged as long as anyone cares about the painting of pictures. Not long ago I asked Frank for a brief statement of his view of Francis for something I was writing – when, after all, his work had long been a target for Bacon's abuse. He sent me the following verse which I am sure still expresses the only feelings that he considers important.

> *You ask me to comment on Francis Bacon;*
> *He has made living images under great provocation.*
> *These images are so eloquent*
> *That further comment would be impertinent.*

I can't remember where I first met Frank but it was probably in '54 or '55. At first I firmly identified him with David Bomberg, a real painter in a very impressive but almost alienating way, who seemed something of a fundamentalist in the way we understand the word now. I had mixed feelings about his famous evening class at the Borough Polytechnic which I had attended, though not at the same time as Frank. I disliked Bomberg's seeming dogmatism and cultivation of acolytes, and I may have thought for a second that Frank was one – but like all acolytes they were the lesser talents. My strongest memory of him in the fifties, though, is undoubtedly of his first show at the Beaux Arts Gallery which, with a few worries that came afterwards and to be brushed aside, I thought a major revelation, and I'm sure that I have never derived a stronger sensation from a contemporary one-man show.

Frank and I soon found that we had, but at different times, been to a very singular boarding school called Bunce Court, near Faversham in Kent. It was 'progressive' and co-educational and had been brought over here lock, stock and barrel from Bavaria by a remarkable woman called Anna Essinger, and for the reason that very nearly all the children and staff were Jewish. I and my brothers and sister were there because our father was that rare phenomenon, a positively Judaeophile British gentile. We were only there for one year, though (1936–7), and therefore missed Frank who arrived alone from Berlin in 1939 and would stay there until 1946. Its unique and rather daunting combination of kindness and austerity must surely have put its stamp on Frank and helped him to realise his most positive innate characteristics – idealism and self-denial combined with an entirely liberal attitude towards others. I am pleased to have caught him laughing in my photograph as he does so very freely though hardly ever at cameras. And while on the subject of laughter I am indebted to him for an evening with the amazing Ken Dodd at the Palladium a couple of years ago and for all sorts of anecdotes and opinions about the theatre on all levels.

In 1975 Frank made a drawing of me. It was an extraordinary experience as he made no attempt, while working on it, to conceal from me the obstinate and anxious uphill struggle needed to give the drawing sufficient validity to be permitted to remain on the slab of super-tough paper (several sheets of hand-made rag paper laminated together). He made and erased about thirty versions before the last was allowed to stay, while I kept my position by focusing on a reproduction of Poussin's *Landscape with a Man Killed by a Snake* on the far wall. It was a good-humoured experience in spite of the tension, and only irksome for me to sit still. Brandy was served at proper (infrequent) intervals. His best drawings as opposed to sketches are surely as resonant in them-selves as his paintings. I recently lived for over a year with a very large one of a mutual friend who lent it to me, and it was a continually inspiring presence in the room that I mainly live and work in.

Frank's struggle as an artist has been longer in practical terms than his thirty years with Marl-borough Fine Art might suggest, but he finally came through, enabling his unceasing struggle with pigment (and compressed charcoal) to continue unburdened with irrelevant worries. He has endured a greater measure of scepticism and incomprehension than most of his peers and has worked more *relentlessly* than any of them except Lucian. His insistence on an almost monastic rigour in his painterly devotions makes me think that he may well be the greatest painter monk since Fra Angelico and certainly the most uxorious since Filippo Lippi (I jest only in part).

I think I met Michael Andrews on the Soho merry and sorry-go-round perhaps a little ear-lier than I did Frank. He was then the thoughtful, dedicated and in his way very ambitious painter that he always has been, but he was also socially quite manic, drinking and behaving with an engaging, and of course entirely sensitive recklessness. All the time he was undoubtedly concerned with complex thoughts about life and work which he would later be able to bring together with such painterly simplicity and intelligence. Frank once said to me 'Mike does these things that at first look like old railway travel posters, but when you really look at them they're just truly beau-tiful pictures'. Well they are of course travel pictures of a very special kind which fulfil their func-tion of making you want to go there and see more of the place, as well as to experience more of the sensibility that supplied your conveyance (not the LNER, though the Norwich School isn't too far way). But I didn't very much *like* his early works, I just felt he had a God-given clue which would definitely lead him somewhere – as it quite soon did.

Because his reclusiveness both in London and the country after he had curtailed his pub and party-going life prevented me from seeing him very often or at will, most meetings with him have

Frank Auerbach in his studio 1986
photo: Bruce Bernard

Leon Kossoff outside Christchurch, Spitalfields 1988
photo: Bruce Bernard

been memorable. In Norwich, we met when he was painting his bold and somehow courageous *Family in the Garden* 1960–62 and I was touring as a backstage worker there with Sadler's Wells Opera. A little later I saw him a few times in Islington when he put me into *The Colony Room* 1962, which at first shocked my humility by making me virtually the central figure, but then wounded my vanity by bringing in Henrietta Moraes to obstruct the view. I went along to see *The Pier Pavilion* (no. 38) almost finished at the studio lent him for a time by the Royal College, having not long before seen the first of his *Lights* series, *Out-of-Doors* (no. 37), even more of a master-piece, illuminating a corridor of very basic power at Rothschild's bank. In 1979 I went deerstalk-ing with him on the Perthshire hills where he had found a new subject matter which he rendered with the familiarity of competent participating and respect for the ritual and the professional stalkers. Nothing is imposed on the experience. There is only the clarity of a moment provided by the camera with a touch of its banality, and the painter's characteristically thoughtful execu-tion and properly simple resolution of his always complex cerebrations. Then Mike painted a small portrait of me in 1990 and this gave me further insight into his painstaking purposefulness as well as making me quite like (no-one else could have done that) my look of somewhat testy disdain. It states as clearly as any portrait I have ever seen how many times is is necessary to look at any-thing in order to paint it as a true study in observation, and in this case to convey it with none of what Francis Bacon, in an almost opposite but related context, called 'its boredom'. But I don't regret the picture's absence here. Just look at the portrait of our one-time friend Tim Behrens (no. 35) which is a great painting as well as a marvellously true study – the apotheosis of a Slade diploma work. He has done many beautiful things since the stalking pictures, and I'm lucky enough, up to the time of writing, to have seen the work on which he is presently engaged – a series on the River Thames which I'm sure will be as beautiful as anything he's done (no. 48).

Not all that long before Francis and I fell out, I asked him exactly what he thought made Mike such an extraordinary painter. His face lit up but he couldn't quite manage it – and who could with a few extempore words? 'It's just his touch I suppose ...' he said, with a smiling acknowl-edgement of his failure.

To conclude this gallimaufry (a word I learned from Lawrence Gowing, one of the staunch-est champions of these artists) of memories and feelings about four painters I have known for so long, I would submit that over that period (though not all this is applicable to Francis) they have shown a more sustained and thoughtful development than the artists of any other country, partly because their overriding impulse seems to have been the pursuit of painterly intelligence rather than the flexing of dubious muscle and submission to the upper artworld / showbiz ethos that still seems so dominant – and it should be emphasised that all of them deplore being considered *champions* of figuration or anyone else's notions of aesthetic morality. Perhaps they are the only ones who have really accepted that today there is perhaps more to *think* about than ever before, and that all progress is now dependent (with passion always present) on an open intelligence, a sense of history as entirely alive, and human feeling nurtured in those lights, rather than the striking of postures, or preaching, or anything which, whether certain artists like it or not, has to get permission from the media to achieve *any* form of existence.

Bearing in mind that Turner, our greatest artist, has not been received anywhere else in the world with quite the honour due to him, and Francis Bacon only in the same equivocal way as in these islands, I think that everyone *in the world* who is interested in the art of painting on this level should ponder the very special qualities of these pictures and their implicit message for the twenty-first century and beyond.

What do I like to think of when considering these four remarkable artists entirely apart from their work?

FRANCIS BACON – *being quite outrageous and funny at Wheeler's in Old Compton Street during the sixties and thereby enslaving the wonderful staff there.*

LUCIAN FREUD – *telling only the best 'have you heard the one abouts', like the one which ends with the artist saying to his model 'Quick, take your clothes off, your husband's coming!' or making his endless and often odious comparisons or coining bizarre but very appropriate descriptive images. Of a rich mean acquaintance who had just had a sudden windfall – '... but he looked as if he'd just* mended *the bank at Monte Carlo!'*

MICHAEL ANDREWS – *imitating both Lucian (almost impossible but I think he's the best) and Francis (everyone does it but he's got some good lines). Opening a bottle of claret with studied but slightly anxious ceremony in case it proves not quite as good as it should be. Listening attentively (and of course appreciatively) to June his wife.*

FRANK AUERBACH – *taking a weekly break (often in the company of his son Jake, and generally on Thursdays) and enjoying an Indian dinner (mostly near Euston Station), all the time talking about painting and poetry and literature and people and the state of the world, as well as laughing quite a lot and sometimes consenting to have an extra drink afterwards in the scruffy pub nearby.*

R. B. Kitaj 1980
photo: David Hockney

Plates

Francis Bacon

1 FIGURE STUDY I 1945–46

2   HEAD VI   1949

3   STUDY FOR SELF-PORTRAIT   1963

4   STUDY FOR PORTRAIT, JULY 1971   1971

Francis
Bacon

5 PORTRAIT OF A MAN WALKING DOWN STEPS 1972

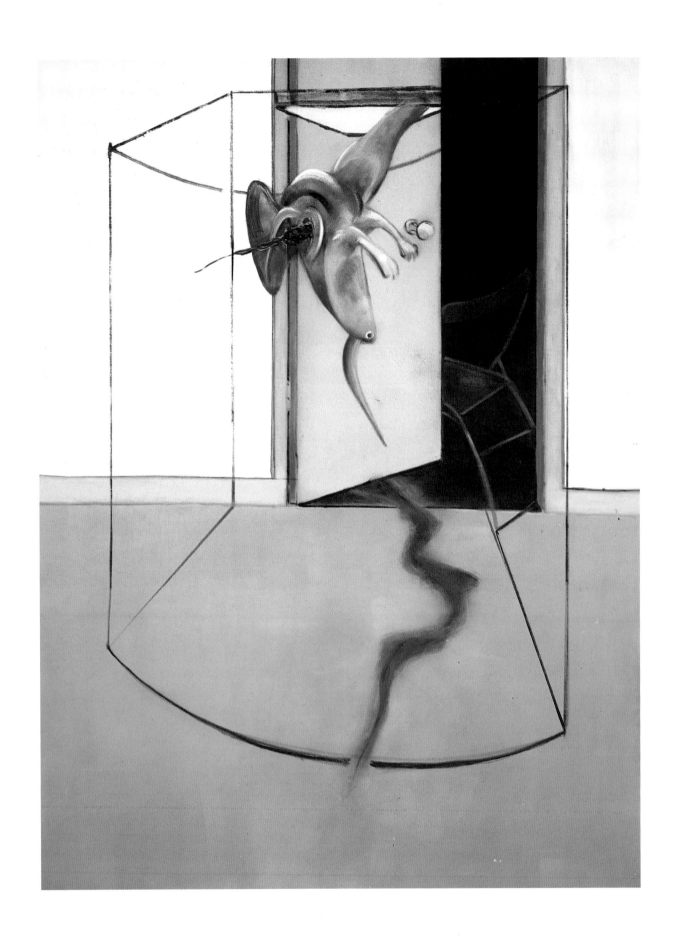

< 6   TRIPTYCH INSPIRED BY THE ORESTEIA OF AESCHYLUS   1981

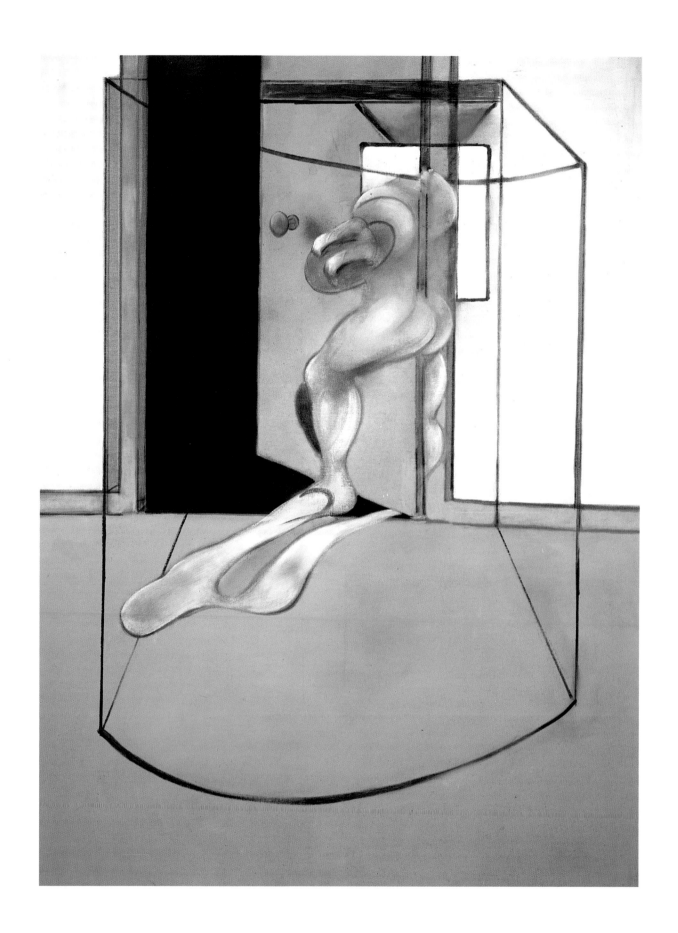

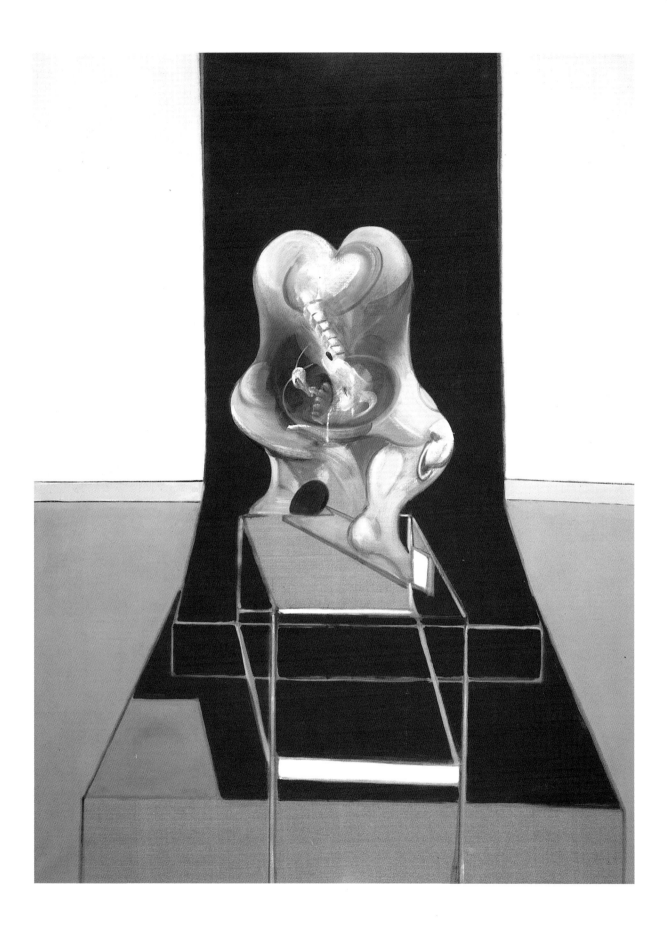

< 7 TRIPTYCH 1983

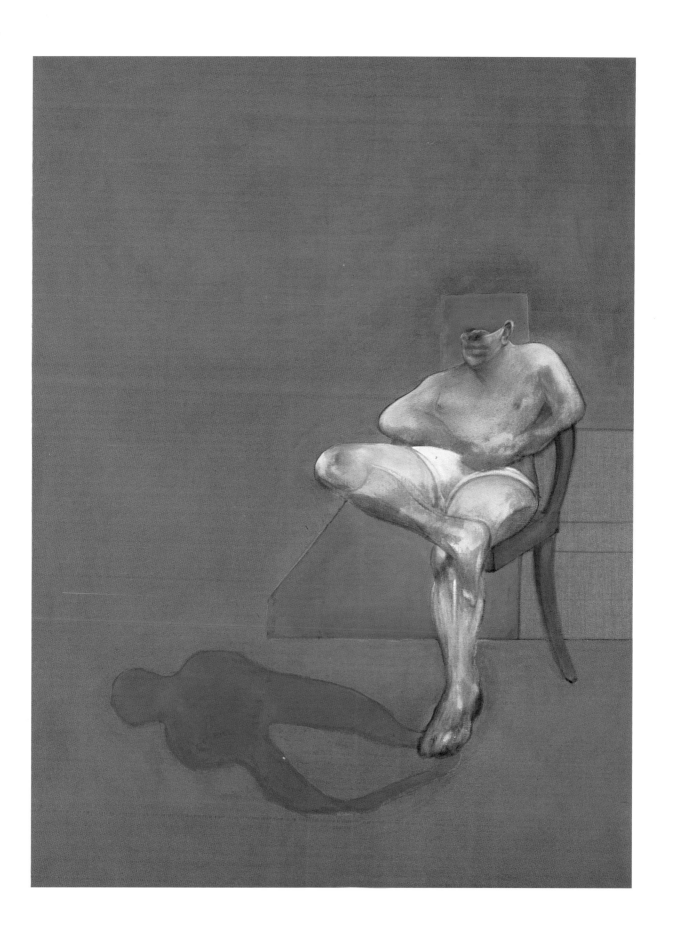

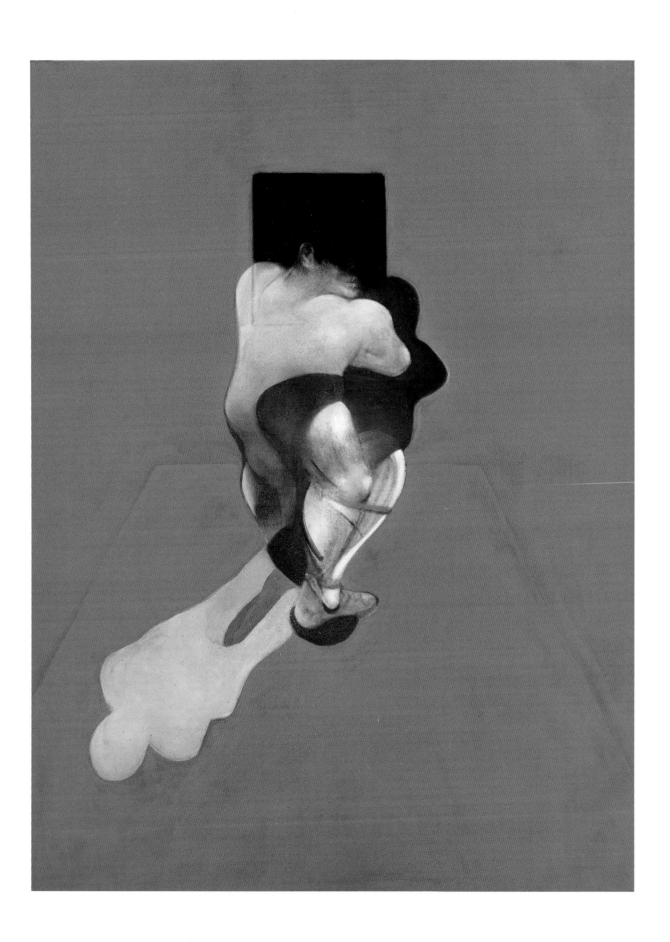

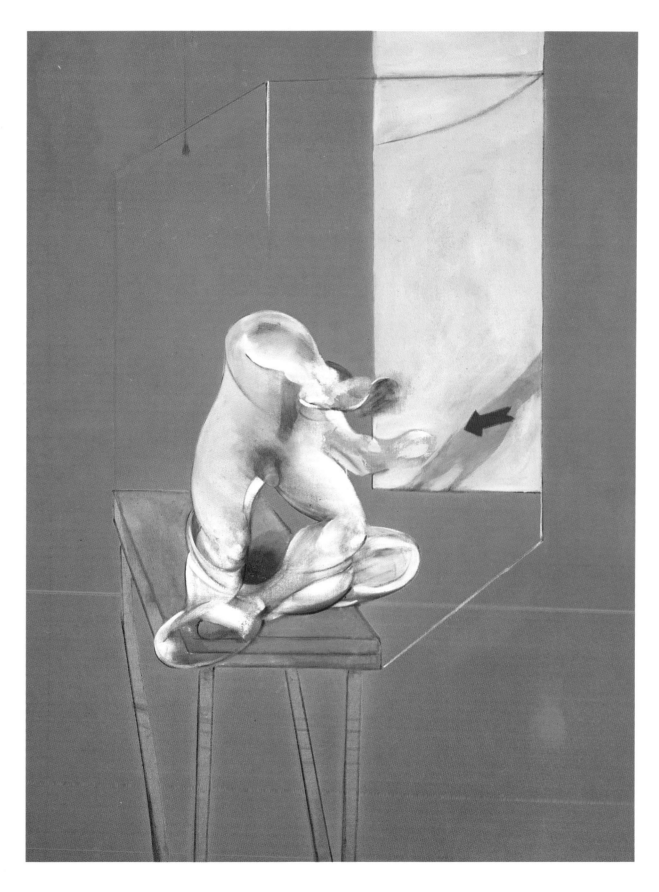

8   STUDY FROM THE HUMAN BODY – FIGURE IN MOVEMENT   1982

Lucian Freud

9 THE VILLAGE BOYS 1942

10   QUINCE ON A BLUE TABLE   1943–44

11 GIRL WITH ROSES 1947–48

12   MAN IN A MACKINTOSH   1957–58

13   A MAN AND HIS DAUGHTER   1963–64

14 WASTEGROUND WITH HOUSES, PADDINGTON 1970–72

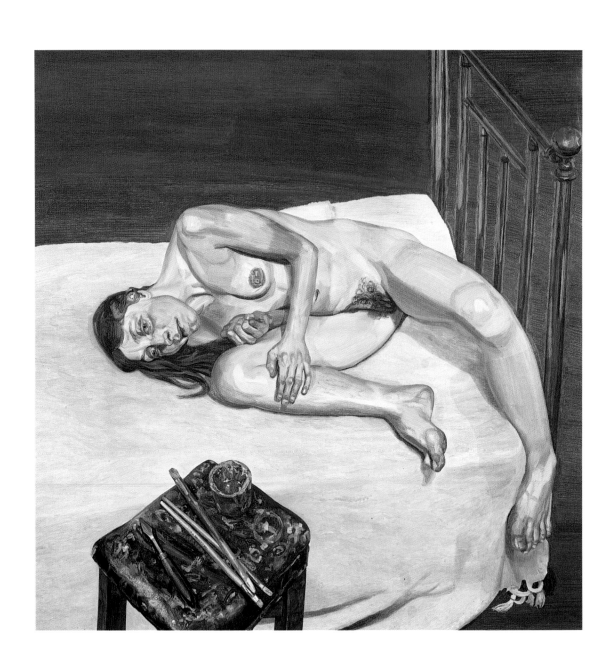

15   NAKED PORTRAIT   1972–73

16 NIGHT PORTRAIT 1977–78

17 NAKED MAN WITH HIS FRIEND 1978–80

18   NAKED PORTRAIT WITH REFLECTION   1980

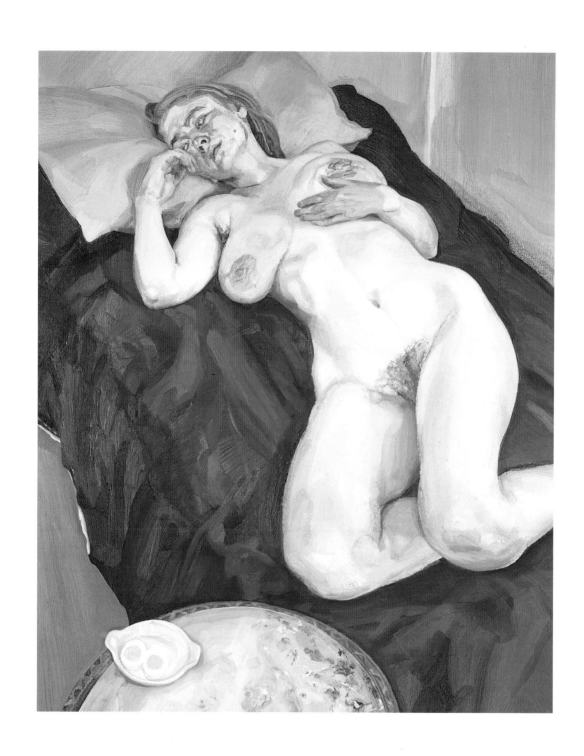

19   NAKED GIRL WITH EGG   1980–81

20 MAN IN A CHAIR 1983–85

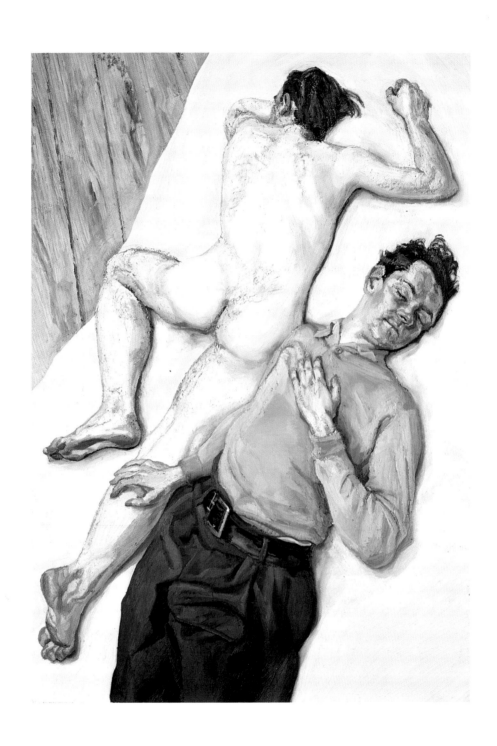

21 TWO MEN 1987–88

22   LYING BY THE RAGS   1989–90

Lucian Freud

23   IB AND HER HUSBAND   1992

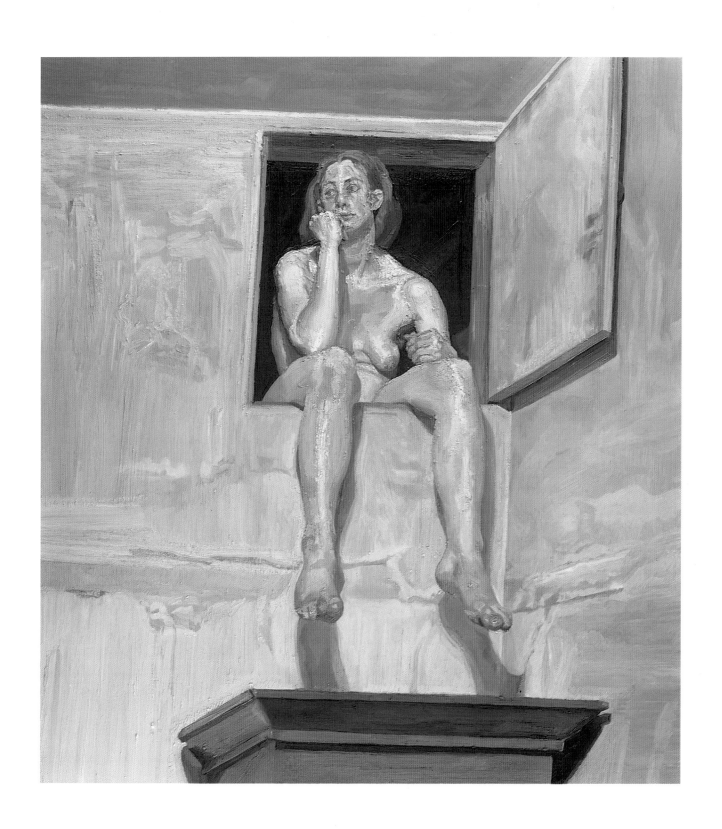

24   GIRL SITTING IN THE ATTIC DOORWAY   1995

Leon Kossoff

25   RAILWAY LANDSCAPE NEAR KING'S CROSS, SUMMER   1967

26   NUDE ON A RED BED, SUMMER   1969

27   FIDELMA NO.2   1981

28   A STREET IN WILLESDEN NO.2   1983

29 PORTRAIT OF CHAIM 1985–86

30   CHRISTCHURCH NO.1. AUGUST 1991   1991

31   CHRISTCHURCH, SPITALFIELDS, EARLY SUMMER   1992

32   FROM WILLESDEN GREEN, SUMMER   1991

33   BETWEEN KILBURN AND WILLESDEN GREEN, WINTER EVENING   1992

34   HEAD OF CHAIM   1993

Michael Andrews

35   TIM BEHRENS   1962

36   PORTRAIT OF JOHN DEAKIN   1963

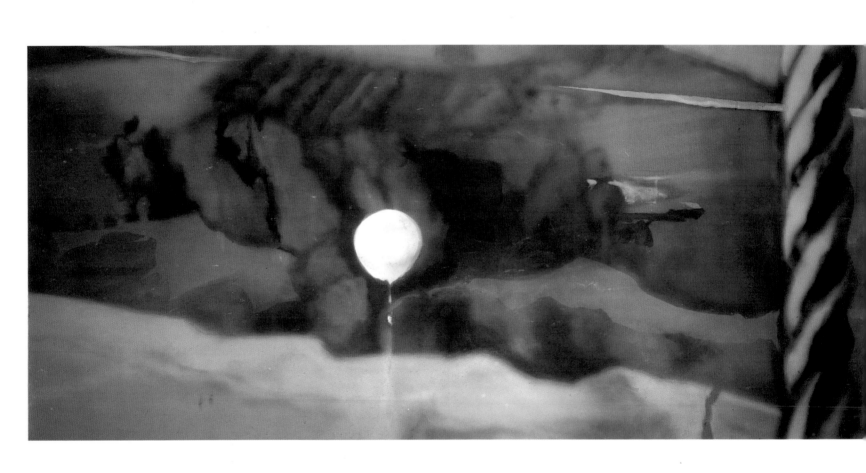

37 LIGHTS I: OUT-OF-DOORS 1970

38   LIGHTS V: THE PIER PAVILION   1973

39   LIGHTS VI: THE SPA   1974

40   THE CATHEDRAL, NORTH EAST FACE, ULURU (AYERS ROCK)   1985

41   VALLEY OF THE WINDS, KATATJUTA (THE OLGAS)   1985–86

42   A VIEW FROM UAMH MHÒR   1990–92

43   THE FOREST BEAT THROUGH A TELESCOPE   1991

44   MIST CLEARING, GLENARTNEY   1991

45   'GIVE ME THE RIFLE...!' 6.30PM, 17TH OCTOBER, GLENARTNEY   1991

46   RECOLLECTION OF A MOMENT IN OCTOBER 1989 –
THE TOBASNICH BURN: GLENARTNEY   1992

47   EDINBURGH (OLD TOWN)   1990–93

micheal Andrews

48   THAMES PAINTING: THE ESTUARY   1994-95

Frank Auerbach

49   HEAD OF E.O.W. IV   1961

50   GAUMONT CINEMA, CAMDEN TOWN   1963

51   PORTRAIT OF HELEN GILLESPIE I   1964

52   MORNINGTON CRESCENT WITH THE STATUE OF SICKERT'S
FATHER-IN-LAW III, SUMMER MORNING   1966

53   THE ORIGIN OF THE GREAT BEAR   1967–68

54   RIMBAUD   1975–76

55 ST PANCRAS STEPS 1978–79

56   HEAD OF J.Y.M. I   1981

57 THE CHIMNEY, MORNINGTON CRESCENT II 1988

58   THE STUDIOS   1993–94

59   HEAD OF DAVID LANDAU   1993–94

60   CATHERINE LAMPERT SEATED   1994

R. B. Kitaj

61 IF NOT, NOT 1975–76

62　BATHER (PSYCHOTIC BOY)　1980

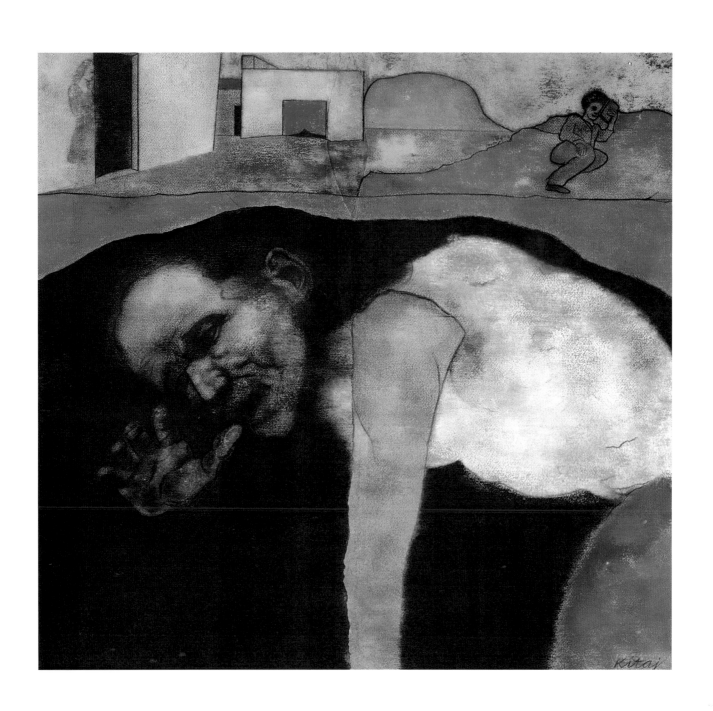

63 THE LISTENER (JOE SINGER IN HIDING) 1980

64 THE ARCHITECTS 1980–84

65   LONDON, ENGLAND (BATHERS)   1982

66   THE JEWISH RIDER   1984–85

67 TWO MESSIAHS 1988

68 WOMEN AND MEN 1991–93

69   WESTERN BATHERS   1993–94

Catalogue and Chronologies

FRANCIS BACON
1909–1992

1   FIGURE STUDY I
1945–46, oil on canvas, 123 × 105.5
Private collection on loan to the Scottish
National Gallery of Modern Art, Edinburgh
Edinburgh only

2   HEAD VI
1949, oil on canvas, 93.2 × 76.5
Arts Council Collection
Edinburgh, Luxembourg and Lausanne

3   STUDY FOR SELF-PORTRAIT
1963, oil on canvas, 165.2 × 142.6
National Museum and Gallery, Cardiff

4   STUDY FOR PORTRAIT, JULY 1971
1971, oil on canvas, 198 × 147.5
Private collection, London
Edinburgh only

5   PORTRAIT OF A MAN WALKING
DOWN STEPS
1972, oil on canvas, 198 × 147.5
Private collection

6   TRIPTYCH INSPIRED BY THE
ORESTEIA OF AESCHYLUS
1981, oil on canvas, each panel 198 × 147.5
Astrup Fearnley Collection

7   TRIPTYCH
1983, oil and pastel on canvas,
each panel 198 × 147.5
Marlborough International Fine Art

8   STUDY FROM THE HUMAN BODY –
FIGURE IN MOVEMENT
1982, oil on canvas, 198 × 147.5
Marlborough International Fine Art

FRANCIS BACON

1909	Born in Dublin, 28 October
1925	Moved to London
1926–28	Travelled to Berlin and then Paris, occasionally receiving commissions for interior decoration and furniture design
1929	Returned to London. Began painting
1941–44	Destroyed nearly all his earlier works
1943	Declared unfit for military service and assigned to Civil Defence (ARP)
1946–50	Lived mainly in Monte Carlo
1950	Settled in London. Taught briefly at the Royal College of Art
1964	Friendship with George Dyer
1971	Death of Dyer
1985	Selected *Artist's Eye* exhibition, National Gallery, London
1992	Died during a visit to Madrid, 28 April

SELECTED SOLO EXHIBITIONS

1949 Hanover Gallery, London
1953 Durlacher Brothers, New York
1955 Institute of Contemporary Arts, London
1957 Galerie Rive Droite, Paris
      Hanover Gallery, London
1960 Marlborough Fine Art, London
1962 Retrospective, Tate Gallery, London, and tour to Mannheim, Turin, Zürich and Amsterdam
1963 Retrospective, Solomon R. Guggenheim Museum, New York, and tour to Chicago
1965 Kunstverein, Hamburg, and tour to Stockholm and Dublin
1971–72 Retrospective, Grand Palais, Paris, and tour to Düsseldorf
1977 Galerie Claude Bernard, Paris
1983 National Museum of Modern Art, Tokyo, and tour to Kyoto and Nagoya
1985–86 Retrospective, Tate Gallery, London, and tour to Stuttgart and Berlin
1988 Central House of Artists, New Tretyakov Gallery, Moscow
1989–90 Hirshhorn Museum and Sculpture Garden, Washington DC, and tour to Los Angeles and New York
1993 Museo Correr, Venice

SELECTED GROUP EXHIBITIONS

1933 Mayor Gallery, London
1937 Agnew's, London
1945 Lefevre Gallery, London
1946 Lefevre Gallery, London
1954 *Nicholson, Bacon and Freud*, British Pavilion, XXVII Venice Biennale
1956 *Masters of British Painting 1800–1950*, Museum of Modern Art, New York
1958 *Three Masters of Modern British Painting: Smith, Pasmore, Bacon*, Arts Council, Victoria Art Gallery, Bath
1959 *V Bienal*, Museu de Arte Moderna, São Paulo

1959 *New Images of Man*, Museum of Modern Art, New York
1960 *Francis Bacon, Hyman Bloom*, University of Los Angeles, Berkeley
1964 *54–64: Painting and Sculpture of a Decade*, Tate Gallery, London
1973 *Cuatro maestros contemporaneos: Giacometti, Dubuffet, De Kooning, Bacon*, Museo de Bellas Artes, Caracas
1976 *The Human Clay*, Hayward Gallery, London
1977 *British Painting 1952–1977*, Royal Academy of Arts, London
      Englische Kunst der Gegenwart, Künstlerhaus, Bregenz
1981 *A New Spirit in Painting*, Royal Academy of Arts, London
      Eight Figurative Painters, Yale Center for British Art, New Haven
1984 *The Hard–Won Image: Traditional Method and Subject in Recent British Art*, Tate Gallery, London
1987 *British Art in the Twentieth Century*, Royal Academy of Arts, London
1987–88 *A School of London: Six Figurative Painters*, British Council touring exhibition to Oslo, Humlebaek, Venice and Düsseldorf
1990 *The Pursuit of the Real: British Figurative Painting from Sickert to Bacon*, Manchester City Art Galleries
1991–92 *From Bacon to Now: The Outsider in British Figuration*, Palazzo Vecchio, Florence
1992–93 *British Figurative Painting of the 20th Century*, Israel Museum, Jerusalem
1994 *Double Reality: 'The School of London'*, Astrup Fearnley Museum of Modern Art, Oslo
1995 *Bacon – Freud: Expressions*, Fondation Maeght, St-Paul de Vence

LUCIAN FREUD
BORN 1922

9 THE VILLAGE BOYS
1942, oil on canvas, 50.8 × 40.6
Private collection
Edinburgh only

10 QUINCE ON A BLUE TABLE
1943–44, oil on canvas, 36.8 × 58.4
Private collection on loan to the Scottish
National Gallery of Modern Art, Edinburgh
Edinburgh only

11 GIRL WITH ROSES
1947–48, oil on canvas, 105.5 × 74.5
The British Council

12 MAN IN A MACKINTOSH
1957–58, oil on canvas, 61 × 61
Private collection

13 A MAN AND HIS DAUGHTER
1963–64, oil on canvas, 61 × 61
Private collection

14 WASTEGROUND WITH HOUSES,
PADDINGTON
1970–72, oil on canvas, 167.5 × 101.5
Private collection

15 NAKED PORTRAIT
1972–73, oil on canvas, 61 × 61
Trustees of the Tate Gallery, London
Edinburgh only

16 NIGHT PORTRAIT
1977–78, oil on canvas, 71.1 × 71.1
Private collection

17 NAKED MAN WITH HIS FRIEND
1978–80, oil on canvas, 90.2 × 105.4
Astrup Fearnley Collection

18 NAKED PORTRAIT WITH
REFLECTION
1980, oil on canvas, 90.3 × 90.3
Private collection
Edinburgh and Luxembourg

19 NAKED GIRL WITH EGG
1980–81, oil on canvas, 75 × 60.5
The British Council

20 MAN IN A CHAIR
1983–85, oil on canvas, 120.7 × 100.4
Thyssen-Bornemisza Collection, Lugano,
Switzerland
Lausanne and Barcelona

21 TWO MEN
1987–88, oil on canvas, 106.7 × 75
Scottish National Gallery of Modern Art,
Edinburgh
Luxembourg, Lausanne and Barcelona

22 LYING BY THE RAGS
1989–90, oil on canvas, 138.5 × 184.2
Astrup Fearnley Collection

23 IB AND HER HUSBAND
1992, oil on canvas, 168 × 147
Private collection
Edinburgh and Luxembourg

24 GIRL SITTING IN THE ATTIC
DOORWAY
1995, oil on canvas, 130.5 × 117.7
Private collection

LUCIAN FREUD

1922 Born in Berlin, 8 December

1933 Moved to London

1938–39 Studied at Central School of Arts and Crafts, London

1939 Acquired British nationality

1939–42 Studied at East Anglian School of Painting and Drawing under Cedric Morris

1942–43 Part-time study at Goldsmiths' College, London

1946–47 Painted in Paris and Greece

1949–54 Visiting tutor, Slade School of Fine Art, London

1951 Arts Council Prize, Festival of Britain

1983 Created a Companion of Honour

1987 Selected *Artist's Eye* exhibition, National Gallery, London

1993 Awarded Order of Merit
Lives in London

SELECTED SOLO EXHIBITIONS

1944 Lefevre Gallery, London

1950 Hanover Gallery, London

1958 Marlborough Fine Art, London

1972 Anthony d'Offay Gallery, London

1974 Retrospective, Hayward Gallery, London, and tour to Bristol, Birmingham and Leeds

1987–88 *Lucian Freud, Paintings*, Hirshhorn Museum and Sculpture Garden, Washington DC, and tour to Paris, London and Berlin (British Council)

1988–89 *Lucian Freud, Works on Paper*, Ashmolean Museum, Oxford, and tour to Edinburgh, Hull, Liverpool, Exeter, San Francisco, Minneapolis, New York, Cleveland and Saint Louis

1988 *Lucian Freud, Paintings 1947–1987*, Scottish National Gallery of Modern Art, Edinburgh

1991–92 *Lucian Freud, Paintings and Works on Paper*, Palazzo Ruspoli, Rome, and tour to Milan, Liverpool, Tochigi, Nishinomiya and Tokyo (British Council)

1992–93 Art Gallery of New South Wales, Sydney, and tour to Perth, Western Australia (British Council)

1993–94 *Lucian Freud: recent work*, Whitechapel Art Gallery, London, and tour to New York and Madrid

SELECTED GROUP EXHIBITIONS

1946 Lefevre Gallery, London

1948 *Forty Years of Modern Art*, Institute of Contemporary Arts, London

1951 *60 Paintings for '51*, Arts Council, for the Festival of Britain

1954 *Nicholson, Bacon and Freud*, British Pavilion, XXVII Venice Biennale

1976 *The Human Clay*, Hayward Gallery, London

1981 *A New Spirit in Painting*, Royal Academy of Arts, London
Eight Figurative Painters, Yale Center for British Art, New Haven

1982 *Aspects of British Art Today*, Tokyo Metropolitan Art Museum

1984 *The Hard-Won Image: Traditional Method and Subject in Recent British Art*, Tate Gallery, London

1987 *British Art in the Twentieth Century*, Royal Academy of Arts, London

1987–88 *A School of London: Six Figurative Painters*, British Council touring exhibition to Oslo, Humlebaek, Venice and Düsseldorf

1990 *The Pursuit of the Real: British Figurative Painting from Sickert to Bacon*, Manchester City Art Galleries

1991–92 *From Bacon to Now: The Outsider in British Figuration*, Palazzo Vecchio, Florence

1992–93 *British Figurative Painting of the 20th Century*, Israel Museum, Jerusalem

1994 *Double Reality: 'The School of London'*, Astrup Fearnley Museum of Modern Art, Oslo

1995 *Bacon – Freud: Expressions*, Fondation Maeght, St-Paul de Vence

LEON KOSSOFF
BORN 1926

25 RAILWAY LANDSCAPE NEAR
KING'S CROSS, SUMMER
1967, oil on board, 122 × 152.4
Ivor Braka Ltd, London

26 NUDE ON A RED BED, SUMMER
1969, oil on board, 77 × 137
Anthony d'Offay Gallery, London

27 FIDELMA NO.2
1981, oil on board, 139.7 × 92.7
Private collection, courtesy L.A. Louver,
Venice, California

28 A STREET IN WILLESDEN NO.2
1983, oil on board, 122 × 167.6
Private collection

29 PORTRAIT OF CHAIM
1985–86, oil on board, 108.6 × 78.1
Private collection, courtesy Anthony d'Offay
Gallery, London

30 CHRISTCHURCH NO.I.
AUGUST 1991
1991, oil on board, 146.7 × 100.4
Collection Ron Burkle, Los Angeles, California

31 CHRISTCHURCH, SPITALFIELDS,
EARLY SUMMER
1992, oil on board, 199.5 × 183
Anthony d'Offay Gallery, London

32 FROM WILLESDEN GREEN,
SUMMER
1991, oil on board, 129 × 108.5
Private collection, courtesy Anthony d'Offay
Gallery, London

33 BETWEEN KILBURN AND WILLES-
DEN GREEN, WINTER EVENING
1992, oil on board, 120 × 148
Scottish National Gallery of Modern Art,
Edinburgh

34 HEAD OF CHAIM
1993, oil on board, 76 × 53
Anthony d'Offay Gallery, London

LEON KOSSOFF

1926 Born in London, 7 December
1945–48 Military service with Royal Fusiliers, attached to 2nd Battalion Jewish Brigade
1949–53 Studied at St Martin's School of Art and under David Bomberg at the Borough Polytechnic, London
1953–56 Studied at the Royal College of Art, London
1959–64 Taught at Chelsea School of Art and the Regent Street Polytechnic, London
1966–69 Taught at St Martin's School of Art
Lives in London

SELECTED SOLO EXHIBITIONS

1957–64 Six exhibitions at the Beaux Arts Gallery, London
1966 Marlborough Fine Art, London
1972 Whitechapel Art Gallery, London
1973 Fischer Fine Art, London
1975 Fischer Fine Art, London
1979 Fischer Fine Art, London
1981 *Leon Kossoff: Paintings from a Decade 1970–1980*, Museum of Modern Art, Oxford
1982 L. A. Louver, Venice, California
1983 Hirschl and Adler Modern, New York
1988 Anthony d'Offay Gallery, London
1993 *Leon Kossoff: Drawings 1985 to 1992*, Anthony d'Offay Gallery, London, and tour to Venice, California
1995 British Pavilion, XLVI Venice Biennale, and tour to Amsterdam

SELECTED GROUP EXHIBITIONS

1964 *54–64: Painting and Sculpture of a Decade*, Tate Gallery, London
1976 *The Human Clay*, Hayward Gallery, London
1977 *British Painting 1952–1977*, Royal Academy of Arts, London
1979–80 *The British Art Show*, Arts Council of Great Britain, Mappin Art Gallery, Sheffield
1984 *The Hard-Won Image: Traditional Method and Subject in Recent British Art*, Tate Gallery, London

1984–85 *The British Art Show*, Arts Council of Great Britain, City of Birmingham Museums and Art Gallery
1987 *British Art in the Twentieth Century*, Royal Academy of Arts, London
Art of our Time, the Saatchi Collection at the Royal Scottish Academy, Edinburgh
1987–88 *A School of London: Six Figurative Painters*, British Council touring exhibition to Oslo, Humlebaek, Venice and Düsseldorf
1989–90 *Leon Kossoff, Bill Woodrow*, Saatchi Collection, London
1990 *The Pursuit of the Real: British Figurative Painting from Sickert to Bacon*, Manchester City Art Galleries
1991–92 *From Bacon to Now: The Outsider in British Figuration*, Palazzo Vecchio, Florence
1992–93 *British Figurative Painting of the 20th Century*, Israel Museum, Jerusalem
1994 *Double Reality: 'The School of London'*, Astrup Fearnley Museum of Modern Art, Oslo

MICHAEL ANDREWS
1928–1995

MICHAEL ANDREWS

1928 Born in Norwich, 30 October
1949–53 Studied at the Slade School of Fine Art, London, under William Coldstream
1953 Received Rome Scholarship in Painting
1959 Taught at Norwich School of Art
1960 Taught at Chelsea School of Art, London
1963–66 Taught at the Slade School of Fine Art
1973 Invited to use Visitor's Studio at the Royal College of Art, London
1975 First visited Scotland
1977–92 Lived in Norfolk
1983 Visited Ayers Rock, Australia
1988–89 Trustee of the National Gallery, London
1992 Returned to London
1995 Died in London, 19 July

SELECTED SOLO EXHIBITIONS

1958 Beaux Arts Gallery, London
1963 Beaux Arts Gallery, London
1974 Anthony d'Offay Gallery, London
1978 Anthony d'Offay Gallery, London
1980–81 Retrospective, Hayward Gallery, London, and tour to Edinburgh and Manchester
1986 *Rock of Ages Cleft for Me: Recent Paintings by Michael Andrews*, Anthony d'Offay Gallery, London
1991 *The Delectable Mountain*, Whitechapel Art Gallery, London, and tour to Paris, Edinburgh and New York
1991 *Michael Andrews: The Scottish Paintings*, Scottish National Gallery of Modern Art, Edinburgh

SELECTED GROUP EXHIBITIONS

1955 *8 Painters*, Institute of Contemporary Arts, London
1963 *British Painting in the Sixties*, Tate Gallery and Whitechapel Art Gallery, London
1964 *54–64: Painting and Sculpture of a Decade*, Tate Gallery, London
1976 *The Human Clay*, Hayward Gallery, London

1977 *British Painting 1952–1977*, Royal Academy of Arts, London
1979–80 *Narrative Painting*, Institute of Contemporary Arts, London
The British Art Show, Arts Council of Great Britain, Mappin Art Gallery, Sheffield
1981 *Eight Figurative Painters*, Yale Center for British Art, New Haven
1984 *The Hard-Won Image: Traditional Method and Subject in Recent British Art*, Tate Gallery, London
Modern Masters from the Thyssen-Bornemisza Collection, Royal Academy of Arts, London
1987 *British Art in the Twentieth Century*, Royal Academy of Arts, London
1987–88 *A School of London: Six Figurative Painters*, British Council touring exhibition to Oslo, Humlebaek, Venice and Düsseldorf
1990 *The Pursuit of the Real: British Figurative Painting from Sickert to Bacon*, Manchester City Art Galleries
1992–93 *British Figurative Painting of the 20th Century*, Israel Museum, Jerusalem
1994 *Double Reality: 'The School of London'*, Astrup Fearnley Museum of Modern Art, Oslo

FRANK AUERBACH
BORN 1931

49 HEAD OF E.O.W. IV
1961, oil on plywood, 59.8 × 56.8
Scottish National Gallery of Modern Art,
Edinburgh

50 GAUMONT CINEMA, CAMDEN
TOWN
1963, oil on board, 89 × 146
Private collection
Edinburgh only

51 PORTRAIT OF HELEN GILLESPIE I
1964, oil on board, 75 × 62.2
Private collection

52 MORNINGTON CRESCENT WITH
THE STATUE OF SICKERT'S
FATHER-IN-LAW III, SUMMER
MORNING
1966, oil on board, 121 × 152.5
Marlborough Fine Art (London) Ltd

53 THE ORIGIN OF THE GREAT BEAR
1967–68, oil on board, 114.6 × 140.2
Trustees of the Tate Gallery, London

54 RIMBAUD
1975–76, oil on board, 107.9 × 107.9
Trustees of the Tate Gallery, London

55 ST PANCRAS STEPS
1978–79, oil on board, 168.2 × 137.5
Rochdale Art Gallery

56 HEAD OF J.Y.M. I
1981, oil on board, 56 × 50.8
Southampton City Art Gallery

57 THE CHIMNEY, MORNINGTON
CRESCENT II
1988, oil on canvas, 153 × 132
Astrup Fearnley Collection

58 THE STUDIOS
1993–94, oil on canvas, 153 × 122.5
Marlborough Fine Art (London) Ltd

59 HEAD OF DAVID LANDAU
1993–94, oil on canvas, 69.8 × 59.7
Marlborough Fine Art (London) Ltd

60 CATHERINE LAMPERT SEATED
1994, oil on board, 61 × 55.9
Private collection

FRANK AUERBACH

1931   Born in Berlin, 29 April
1939   Sent to England
1947   Acquired British nationality
      Moved to London
1948–52   Studied at St Martin's School of Art and under David Bomberg at the Borough Polytechnic, London
1952–55   Studied at the Royal College of Art, London
1956–68   Taught part-time at the Sidcup, Ealing, Bromley, Camberwell and Slade Schools of Art
      Lives in London

SELECTED SOLO EXHIBITIONS

1956–63   Five exhibitions at the Beaux Arts Gallery, London
1965   Marlborough Fine Art, London
1969   Marlborough–Gerson Gallery, New York
1971   Marlborough Fine Art, London
1978   Retrospective, Hayward Gallery, London, and tour to Edinburgh
1986   British Pavilion, XLII Venice Biennale
1986–87   Kunstverein, Hamburg, and tour to Essen and Madrid
1989   Rijksmuseum Vincent Van Gogh, Amsterdam
1990   Marlborough Fine Art, London

SELECTED GROUP EXHIBITIONS

1958   *The Pittsburgh International*, Carnegie Institute, Pittsburgh
1963   *British Painting in the Sixties*, Tate Gallery and Whitechapel Art Gallery, London
1968   *Helen Lessore and the Beaux Arts Gallery*, Marlborough Fine Art, London
1976   *The Human Clay*, Hayward Gallery, London
1981   *A New Spirit in Painting*, Royal Academy of Arts, London
      Eight Figurative Painters, Yale Center for British Art, New Haven

1982   *Aspects of British Art Today*, Tokyo Metropolitan Art Museum
1984   *The Hard-Won Image: Traditional Method and Subject in Recent British Art*, Tate Gallery, London
1984–85   *The British Art Show*, Arts Council of Great Britain, City of Birmingham Museums and Art Gallery
1987   *British Art in the Twentieth Century*, Royal Academy of Arts, London
      Current Affairs: British Sculpture and Painting in the 1980s, Museum of Modern Art, Oxford
      Art of our Time, the Saatchi Collection at the Royal Scottish Academy, Edinburgh
1987–88   *A School of London: Six Figurative Painters*, British Council touring exhibition to Oslo, Humlebaek, Venice and Düsseldorf
1990   *The Pursuit of the Real: British Figurative Painting from Sickert to Bacon*, Manchester City Art Galleries
      Chagall to Kitaj: Jewish Experience in 20th Century Art, Barbican Art Gallery, London
1991–92   *From Bacon to Now: The Outsider in British Figuration*, Palazzo Vecchio, Florence
1992–93   *British Figurative Painting of the 20th Century*, Israel Museum, Jerusalem
1994   *Double Reality: 'The School of London'*, Astrup Fearnley Museum of Modern Art, Oslo

R. B. KITAJ
BORN 1932

61 IF NOT, NOT
1975–76, oil and black chalk on canvas,
152.4 × 152.4
Scottish National Gallery of Modern Art,
Edinburgh

62 BATHER (PSYCHOTIC BOY)
1980, pastel and charcoal on paper, 134 × 57.2
Astrup Fearnley Collection

63 THE LISTENER (JOE SINGER
IN HIDING)
1980, pastel and charcoal on paper, 103.2 × 108.2
Private collection

64 THE ARCHITECTS
1980–84, oil on canvas, 152.4 × 121.9
M. J. Long
Edinburgh only

65 LONDON, ENGLAND (BATHERS)
1982, oil on canvas, 152.4 × 121.9
Private collection

66 THE JEWISH RIDER
1984–85, oil on canvas, 152.4 × 152.4
Astrup Fearnley Collection

67 TWO MESSIAHS
1988, oil on canvas, 244 × 76
Astrup Fearnley Collection

68 WOMEN AND MEN
1991–93, oil on canvas, 153.3 × 153.3
Marlborough Fine Art (London) Ltd

69 WESTERN BATHERS
1993–94, oil on canvas, 127.3 × 195.9
Marlborough Fine Art (London) Ltd

R.B.KITAJ

1932 Born in Cleveland, Ohio, 29 October
1950–51 Studied at the Cooper Union Institute, New York
1951–52 Studied at the Akademie der Bildenden Künste, Vienna
1952–53 Further study at the Cooper Union Institute
1957–59 Studied at the Ruskin School of Drawing, Oxford
1959–61 Studied at the Royal College of Art, London
1967–68 Taught at the University of California, Berkeley
1970–71 Taught at the University of California, Los Angeles
1976 Selected *The Human Clay* exhibition for the Arts Council
1978–79 Artist-in-Residence, Dartmouth College, New Hampshire
1980 Selected *Artist's Eye* exhibition, National Gallery, London
1981–82 Lived in Paris
1985 Elected to the Royal Academy of Arts
1989 Published *First Diasporist Manifesto* Lives in London

SELECTED SOLO EXHIBITIONS

1963 *R.B. Kitaj: Pictures with Commentary, Pictures without Commentary*, Marlborough Fine Art, London
1965 Marlborough-Gerson Gallery, New York
     Los Angeles County Museum of Art
1967 Cleveland Museum of Art, Ohio
1969 *R.B. Kitaj: complete graphics 1963–69*, Galerie Mikro, Berlin, and tour to Stuttgart, Munich, Düsseldorf, Lübeck and Bonn
1970 Kestner-Gesellschaft, Hanover, and tour to Rotterdam
1974 Marlborough Gallery, New York
1975 *R.B. Kitaj: pictures*, New 57 Gallery, Edinburgh
1977 Marlborough Fine Art, London
1980 Marlborough Fine Art, London

1981 Hirshhorn Museum and Sculpture Garden, Washington DC, and tour to Cleveland and Düsseldorf
1985 Marlborough Fine Art, London, and tour to New York
1994–95 *R. B. Kitaj: A Retrospective*, Tate Gallery, London, and tour to Los Angeles and New York

SELECTED GROUP EXHIBITIONS

1963 *British Painting in the Sixties*, Tate Gallery and Whitechapel Art Gallery, London
1964 *54–64: Painting and Sculpture of a Decade*, Tate Gallery, London
1969 *Information*, Badischer Kunstverein, Karlsruhe
1973 *Dine, Kitaj*, Cincinnati Art Museum
1976 *Peter Blake, Richard Hamilton, David Hockney, R. B. Kitaj, Eduardo Paolozzi*, Museum Boymans-van Beuningen, Rotterdam
     Arte inglese oggi, Palazzo Reale, Milan
1977 *Hayward Annual*, Arts Council of Great Britain, London
1981 *A New Spirit in Painting*, Royal Academy of Arts, London
1984 *The Hard-Won Image: Traditional Method and Subject in Recent British Art*, Tate Gallery, London
1987 *British Art in the Twentieth Century*, Royal Academy of Arts, London
1987–88 *A School of London: Six Figurative Painters*, British Council touring exhibition to Oslo, Humlebaek, Venice and Düsseldorf
1990 *Chagall to Kitaj: Jewish Experience in 20th Century Art*, Barbican Art Gallery, London
1991 *Pop Art*, Royal Academy of Arts, London
1992 *From Bacon to Now: The Outsider in British Figuration*, Palazzo Vecchio, Florence
1993 *British Figurative Painting of the 20th Century*, Israel Museum, Jerusalem
1994 *Double Reality: 'The School of London'*, Astrup Fearnley Museum of Modern Art, Oslo

Prints

Dimensions are plate (or printed image) size. Where two dates are given for prints by Leon Kossoff, the first records execution, the second publication

LUCIAN FREUD

70 BLOND GIRL
1985, etching, 69 × 54.2
Private collection

71 MAN POSING
1985, etching, 70 × 55
Private collection

72 GIRL HOLDING HER FOOT
1985, etching, 69 × 54
Scottish National Gallery of Modern Art, Edinburgh

73   GIRL SITTING
1987, etching, 52.7 × 69.9
Scottish National Gallery of Modern Art,
Edinburgh

74   NAKED MAN ON A BED
1990, etching, 29.8 × 29.8
Private collection

75   KAI
1991–92, etching, 69.5 × 54.5
Private collection

76   THE EGYPTIAN BOOK
1994, etching, 30 × 30
Scottish National Gallery of Modern Art,
Edinburgh

77   RECLINING FIGURE
1994, etching, 17 × 24.5
Scottish National Gallery of Modern Art,
Edinburgh

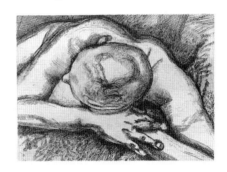

LEON KOSSOFF

78   CHAIM
1986/92, drypoint, 50.6 × 41.7
Private collection

79 FIDELMA
1986/92, drypoint, 50.4 × 42.9
Private collection

80 A STREET IN WILLESDEN
1986/92, drypoint, 64.4 × 49.4
Private collection

81 CHRISTCHURCH, SPRING
1989/92, etching, 59.4 × 40.5
Private collection

82 PILAR AND JACINTO NO.2
1992, drypoint, 47.6 × 37.8
Private collection

83 PILAR AND JACINTO NO.3
1992, drypoint, 50.7 × 45.5
Private collection

84 FIDELMA AND EOIN NO.1
1992, drypoint, 51 × 44.3
Private collection

FRANK AUERBACH

SIX ETCHINGS OF HEADS 1980-81

85 JOE TILSON
15 × 13.5
Marlborough Graphics Ltd

86 R.B.KITAJ
15 × 13.5
Marlborough Graphics Ltd

87 LEON KOSSOFF
15 × 13.5
Marlborough Graphics Ltd

88 LUCIAN FREUD
15 × 13.5
Marlborough Graphics Ltd

89 GERDA BOEHM
15 × 13.5
Marlborough Graphics Ltd

90 JULIA
13.5 × 15
Marlborough Graphics Ltd

91 RUTH I
1994, etching, 25 × 20.2
Marlborough Graphics Ltd

92 RUTH II
1994, etching, 25 × 20.2
Marlborough Graphics Ltd

R. B. KITAJ

93 SELF PORTRAIT (COLD IN PARIS)
1982, soft ground etching, 34.8 × 26.4
Marlborough Graphics Ltd

94 SELF PORTRAIT (AFTER MATTEO)
1983, etching, 46.6 × 35
Marlborough Graphics Ltd

95 SELF PORTRAIT (HAND ON CHIN)
1983, soft ground etching, 32.2 × 24.2
Marlborough Graphics Ltd

96 SELF PORTRAIT (READING)
1983, etching, 49.4 × 37.0
Marlborough Graphics Ltd

97 SELF PORTRAIT
1991, lithograph, 70 × 57
Marlborough Graphics Ltd

98 MY MOTHER I
1991, etching, 16 × 10
Marlborough Graphics Ltd

99 MY MOTHER II
1991, etching, 10 × 16
Marlborough Graphics Ltd

Selected Bibliography

GENERAL

Robertson, Russell, Snowdon, *Private View*,
Edinburgh 1965

The Forgotton Fifties, Graves Art Gallery, Sheffield
1984

Richard Morphet, *The Hard-Won Image: Traditional
Method and Subject in Recent British Art*, Tate
Gallery, London 1984

Helen Lessore, *A Partial Testament: Essays on Some
Moderns in the Great Tradition*, London 1986

Susan Compton (ed.), *British Art in the 20th Century:
The Modern Movement*, Royal Academy, London
1987

A School of London: Six Figurative Painters, British
Council, London 1987

Michael Peppiatt, 'Could there be a School of
London?', *Art International*, Autumn 1987

Tim Wilcox (ed.), *The Pursuit of the Real: British
Figurative Painting from Sickert to Bacon*,
Manchester City Art Galleries 1990

Edward Lucie-Smith, 'British Art in the Twentieth
Century' in *The British Imagination*, Hirschl &
Adler Galleries, New York 1991

Yigal Zalmona (ed.), *British Figurative Painting of the
20th Century*, Israel Museum and British Council
1992

*Seven British Painters: Selected Masters of Post-War
British Art*, Marlborough Fine Art, London 1993

Helen Lessore, Artist and Art Dealer, Theo Waddington
Fine Art, London 1994

MICHAEL ANDREWS

David Sylvester, 'Michael Andrews', *The Listener*, 16
January 1958

Michael Andrews, 'Notes and Preoccupations', *X: A
Quarterly Review*, Volume One, no.2, March 1960

Victor Willing, 'Morality and the Model', interview
with Michael Andrews, *Art and Literature*, Paris,
summer 1964

Michael Andrews, Statement in *Survey 66: Figurative
Art*, Camden Art Centre 1966

John Rothenstein, *Modern English Painters*, Volume
III, London 1974

William Feaver, 'Stranded Dinosaurs', *London
Magazine*, July / August 1978

Anne Seymour, Introduction, *Michael Andrews:
Paintings 1977–78*, Anthony d'Offay Gallery,
London 1978

Lawrence Gowing, Catherine Lampert, *Michael
Andrews*, Hayward Gallery, London 1980

William Feaver, Introduction, *Rock of Ages Cleft for
Me*, Anthony d'Offay Gallery, London 1986

Bruce Bernard, Jonathan Raban, *Michael Andrews:
'The Delectable Mountain'*, Whitechapel Art
Gallery, London 1991

Richard Calvocoressi, *Michael Andrews: The Scottish
Paintings*, Scottish National Gallery of Modern
Art, Edinburgh 1991

FRANK AUERBACH

Michael Podro, Introduction, *Frank Auerbach*, Marlborough-Gerson Gallery, New York 1969

William Feaver, Introduction, *Frank Auerbach*, Marlborough Galerie, Zurich 1976

Leon Kossoff, Foreword to retrospective catalogue, *Frank Auerbach*, Hayward Gallery, London 1978

Catherine Lampert, 'A conversation with Frank Auerbach' in *Frank Auerbach*, Hayward Gallery, London 1978

Stephen Spender, Introduction, *Frank Auerbach*, Marlborough Gallery Inc, New York 1982

Catherine Lampert, 'Frank Auerbach' in *Frank Auerbach, Paintings and Drawings 1977–1985*, XLII Venice Biennale, British Council, London 1986

Mel Gooding, 'The Phenomenon of Presence' in *Frank Auerbach: Recent Work*, Rijksmuseum Vincent Van Gogh, Amsterdam 1989

Michael Podro, Introduction, *Frank Auerbach: The Complete Etchings 1954–1990*, Marlborough Graphics, London 1990

Robert Hughes, *Frank Auerbach*, London 1990

Peter Ackroyd, Introduction, *Frank Auerbach: Recent Works*, Marlborough Gallery, New York 1994

FRANCIS BACON

Roland Penrose, David Sylvester, *Francis Bacon*, Galerie Rive Droite, Paris 1957

Ronald Alley, John Rothenstein, *Francis Bacon*, Tate Gallery, London 1962

Lawrence Alloway, *Francis Bacon*, Solomon R. Guggenheim Museum, New York 1963

Ronald Alley and John Rothenstein, *Francis Bacon*, London 1964

David Sylvester, *Interviews with Francis Bacon*, London 1975 and subsequent editions

John Russell, *Francis Bacon*, London 1971, rev. 1979

Gilles Deleuze, *Francis Bacon: Logique de la Sensation*, Paris 1981

Michel Leiris, *Francis Bacon, Full Face and in Profile*, Oxford and New York 1983

Andrew Forge, Dawn Ades, *Francis Bacon*, Tate Gallery, London 1985

Lawrence Gowing, Sam Hunter, *Francis Bacon*, London and Washington 1989

Achille Bonito Oliva (ed.), David Sylvester, David Mellor, Gilles Deleuze, Lorenza Trucchi, Daniel Palazzoli, *Francis Bacon*, Museo Correr, Venice 1993

Jean Clair, 'Le pathos et la mort', interview with Francis Bacon, in *Corps Crucifiés*, Reunion des Musées Nationaux, Paris 1993

LUCIAN FREUD

Lucian Freud, 'Some thoughts on painting', *Encounter*, July 1954

John Russell, Introduction, *Lucian Freud*, Hayward Gallery, London 1974

John Rothenstein, *Modern English Painters*, Volume III, London 1974

Lawrence Gowing, *Lucian Freud*, London 1982

Robert Hughes, 'On Lucian Freud' in *Lucian Freud Paintings*, British Council, London 1987

Nicholas Penny, 'The Early Works 1938–54' in *Lucian Freud, Works on Paper*, South Bank Centre, London 1988

Catherine Lampert, *Lucian Freud: recent work*, Whitechapel Art Gallery, London 1993

William Feaver, 'Beyond Feeling' in *Lucian Freud*, Art Gallery of New South Wales, Sydney 1993

Craig Hartley, *The Etchings of Lucian Freud: a catalogue raisonné 1946–1995*, London 1995

R.B.KITAJ

Timothy Hyman, 'A Return to London', interview with R. B. Kitaj, *London Magazine*, February 1980

R. B. Kitaj, 'School of London' in *The Human Clay*, Arts Council of Great Britain, London 1976

Robert Creeley, 'Ecce Homo' in *R. B. Kitaj: Pictures/Bilder*, Marlborough Fine Art, London & Zurich 1977

Timothy Hyman, 'R. B. Kitaj: Decadence and Renewal' in *R. B. Kitaj: Fifty Drawings and Pastels, Six Oil Paintings*, Marlborough Gallery, New York 1979

Stephen Spender, Introduction, *R. B. Kitaj: Pastels and Drawings*, Marlborough Fine Art, London 1980

John Ashbery, Joe Shannon, Jane Livingston, Timothy Hyman, *R. B. Kitaj: paintings, drawings, pastels*, London 1983

Marco Livingstone, *R. B. Kitaj*, Oxford 1985

David Cohen, 'R. B. Kitaj and the Art of Return', *Jewish Quarterly*, July 1988

Timothy Hyman, *R. B. Kitaj: The Sensualist 1973–84*, Oslo 1991

Richard Morphet (ed.), Richard Wollheim, R. B. Kitaj, *R. B. Kitaj: A Retrospective*, Tate Gallery, London 1994

Jane Kinsman, *R. B. Kitaj's Prints*, Aldershot 1994

LEON KOSSOFF

John Berger, 'The Weight', *New Statesman*, 19 September 1959

David Mercer, Introduction, *Leon Kossoff: Recent Paintings*, Whitechapel Art Gallery, London 1972

Peter Fuller, 'Leon Kossoff', *Art Monthly*, London May 1979

Marina Vaizey, 'Leon Kossoff', *Art International*, Volume XXIII, September 1979

David Elliott, Introduction, *Leon Kossoff: Paintings from a Decade 1970–1980*, Museum of Modern Art, Oxford 1981

Lawrence Gowing, 'Here Comes the Diesel' in *Leon Kossoff*, Anthony d'Offay Gallery, London 1988

James Hyman, 'The Prints of Leon Kossoff', *Print Quarterly*, X, 1993

David Sylvester, Rudi Fuchs, Leon Kossoff, *Leon Kossoff*, British Pavilion, XLVI Venice Biennale, British Council 1995

LENDERS

Anthony d'Offay Gallery 26, 31, 34
Arts Council Collection 2
Astrup Fearnley Collection 6, 17, 22, 36, 40, 41, 57, 62, 66, 67
Ivor Braka Ltd 25
The British Council 11, 19, 46
Ron Burkle, Los Angeles 30
M. J. Long 64
Marlborough Fine Art (London) Ltd 52, 58, 59, 68, 69
Marlborough Graphics Ltd 85, 86, 87, 88, 89, 90, 91, 92, 93, 94, 95, 96, 97, 98, 99
Marlborough International Fine Art 7, 8
National Museum and Gallery, Cardiff 3
Private collections 1, 4, 5, 9, 10, 12, 13, 14, 16, 18, 23, 24, 27, 28, 29, 32, 39, 42, 43, 44, 45, 48, 50, 51, 60, 63, 65, 70, 71, 74, 75, 78, 79, 80, 81, 82, 83, 84
Scottish National Gallery of Modern Art, Edinburgh 21, 33, 47, 49, 61, 72, 73, 76, 77
Tate Gallery 15, 53, 54
Rochdale Art Gallery 55
Southampton City Art Gallery 56
Thyssen-Bornemisza Collection, Lugano 20
Fundación Colección Thyssen-Bornemisza, Madrid 35, 38

PHOTOGRAPHIC CREDITS

Acquavella Galleries; Anthony d'Offay Gallery; Arts Council Collection; Astrup Fearnley Museum of Modern Art, Oslo; Kaare Berntsen, Oslo; Ivor Braka Ltd; Bridgeman Art Library; The British Council; Gerry Clist Photography; Prudence Cuming Associates Ltd; Matthew Hollow; L. A. Louver, California; Marlborough Fine Art (London) Ltd; Marlborough Graphics Ltd; Marlborough International Fine Art; Antonia Reeve; John Riddy; Rochdale Art Gallery; Scottish National Gallery of Modern Art, Edinburgh; Southampton City Art Gallery; Tate Gallery; Thyssen-Bornemisza Collection, Lugano; Fundación Colección Thyssen-Bornemisza, Madrid; Peter Wood.